BUILD TO WIN

BUILD TO WIN

Composite material technology for competition cars and motorcycles

Keith Noakes

Foreword by Eric Broadley

OSPREY

First published in 1988 by Osprey Publishing
59 Grosvenor Street, London W1X 9DA
Reprinted summer 1989

Sole distributors in the USA

Osceola, Wisconsin 54020, USA

British Library Cataloguing in Publication Data

Noakes, Keith
    Build to win.
    1. Racing cars. Composite materials. Use.
    2. Racing motorcycles. Composite materials.
    Use.
    I. Title
    629.2'28

ISBN 0–85045–826–9

Editor Tony Thacker
Design Simon Bell

Filmset and printed in England by
Butler & Tanner Ltd, Frome and London

Contents

Acknowledgements 7
Foreword 9
Introduction 10

Part One – The history and use of composites

1 Early developments 13
2 Phenolic- and epoxy-resin systems 17
3 Fibre technology 20
4 Process methods 25

Part Two – Composites in competition cars

1 Summary 39
2 Benetton Formula 46
3 Cooper 52
4 Ferrari 54
5 Ford UFO 2 Project 59
6 TWR Jaguar 61
7 Lola Cars 66
8 Team Lotus 71
9 McLaren 75
10 Motor Racing Developments (Brabham) 81
11 Reynard Racing 84
12 Williams GP Engineering 87

Part Three – Composites in competition motorcycles

1 Summary   97
2 Armstrong Competition Motorcycles   102
3 Ducati   104
4 Honda   107
5 Gallina Suzuki   110
6 Heron Suzuki   111
7 A European composite motorcycle project   116
8 The Wheatley Lingham 500   117

Part Four – Postscript

1 Composite structure safety   121
2 Conclusion   124

Index   125

Acknowledgements

The author would like to acknowledge and thank the companies and persons listed below who were an invaluable help in supplying photographs, information and checking for detail accuracy.

CIBA-GEIGY Bonded Structures
Williams GP Engineering
Ferrari
McLaren International
Motor Racing Developments
Benetton
Team Lotus
Lola Cars
Reynard Racing
Heron Suzuki
Armstrong Competition Motorcycles
Richard Francis Action Plus
Motorcycle News
Patrick Head
John Barnard
Harvey Postlethwaite
Eric Broadley
Peter Warr
Gordon Murray
Nigel Leaper
Mike Eatough
Jonathan Greaves
Brian O'Rorke
Martin Ogilvie
Gordon Coppuck
Phillip Henderson
Paul Owens
Don Morley
Alan Cathcart
Peter Clifford
Gary Lingham
Chris Wheatley
Malcolm Bryan

Foreword by Eric Broadley

Autosport, in all its forms, has been, and always will be, very competitive, not only for the competitors themselves, but also for the designers and builders of the machinery with which they compete. In many years of designing and building racing cars for a variety of different formulae, the quest for a technical advantage has never ceased.

An example of the introduction of a new concept was when the tubular space frame had reached the practical limit of its development, and the single-skin aluminium monocoque replaced it. This dramatic and very different looking concept was to become the standard method of chassis construction for many different formulae, but dramatic as it was, the monocoque was still made from a very conventional material, aluminium.

The use of composites in the design and construction of competition vehicles, as shown in this book, was probably the most dramatic change ever. Not only are the materials and their process methods entirely different to conventional materials, but so are their performance details. The designer has been faced with utilizing materials that are totally different in every respect from those used before, and with no previous designs as reference, or benchmarks, only the material manufacturers' individual data sheets as guides.

Many race-car designers are now totally dependent on the use of composites, from the structural chassis to the bodywork, and it would be impossible to consider their designs without composite materials. The immense technical potential gained from the use of composites has produced cars of both advanced performance and great safety.

Composites have revolutionized competition-vehicle design, and great advances have been made since these materials became available. One person who has witnessed all of these advances is Keith Noakes who, as technical representative of one of the world's foremost composite suppliers, has worked closely with most of the leading teams from the very beginning. With this book, he makes it possible for the enthusiast to understand something about composites and their progress in the design and building of competition cars and motorcycles.

Eric Broadley
Lola Cars

Eric Broadley of Lola Cars with one of the many cars that have established the company as a front-runner in motor sport

Introduction

This book aims to give an outline history of the use of composites in competition cars and motorcycles, coupled with individual case histories, but does not intend to be a complete historical record or to cover every individual application. Therefore, to those readers, designers and users who feel their particular application is not covered by this book, the author makes his apologies.

Composites, in some form or other, have probably been used for engineering purposes since Egyptian times, but composites as we now know them, and as covered by this book, are far more modern.

These modern forms of composites began with the use of phenol-based adhesives for metal-to-metal bonding, used in late World War 2 and early post-war aircraft. The war years also saw the development in England, at Aero Research of Duxford, of a material called Gordon Aerolight. This consisted of flax fibres impregnated with a modified phenolic resin, which was formed in a mould or press, cured under pressure and heated to form a tough, durable, non-metallic structure.

When there was a fear of aluminium running short for aircraft production, a Spitfire fuselage was constructed from Gordon Aerolight for test purposes, although it never actually reached a complete aircraft. However, tests by the Royal Aircraft Establishment did show that this fuselage met the required specifications.

This book is about competition cars and motorcycles, neither of which were to utilize composites to any serious or notable degree until several years after World War 2.

In recent years, the major advances in composite research and development have taken place in Europe and the USA, which is also where the major strides have taken place in the use of these materials for competition cars and motorcycles. They have had a revolutionary effect on competition vehicles of all types, allowing designers to produce immensely strong, yet light, structures that ensure excellent performance in terms of speed, handling and road-holding. Furthermore, they offer a degree of driver safety far above that of previously used conventional materials.

Without doubt, the future of competition car and motorcycle design lies in the use of composites, and this extremely competitive industry will take the development of those materials to the limit.

Keith Noakes
March 1988

Part One   The history and use of composites

1 Early developments
2 Phenolic- and epoxy-resin systems
3 Fibre technology
4 Process methods

1   Early developments

Glass-reinforced plastic

Composites in the true sense, that is, being used for technical reasons, began with the advent of fibreglass and polyester matrix resins. Fibreglass first became available in the early 1950s; its ease of use and versatility soon found it being widely used for many and various applications. This combination of polyester resin and glass was a technical breakthrough. The term GRP (glass-reinforced plastic) was born and is still the universal description.

These new materials were utilized in non-structural areas, such as fairings, ducting, and very soon bodywork also. Complex aerodynamic shapes could be produced very quickly and cheaply, and with limited skill.

The basic method consisted of producing a master shape, or buck; this shape could be made from wood, plaster, etc—the choice of materials was dependent on cost and available skills. Whatever the component, though, small or large, the method was the same: a master was produced, then moulds were taken from it, either in plaster-type materials or the now-available polyester resins. The method of utilizing the polyester consisted of mixing two components—a resin and a hardener, usually in a brushable consistency.

The mould, having been treated with a release agent, would have a wet coat of resin applied by brush or spray, a layer of glass fibre, either woven or in a random-fibre mat, was laid on to the wet resin, more resin was applied, rollers and squeezes were used to force the resin to wet out the glass fibre. The required thickness or strength was controlled by the number of layers used.

This type of construction soon became known as the wet lay-up method, a term still used. One of the shortcomings of this form of construction was that, in order to achieve the required strength, the number of laminates in many cases caused a weight penalty. Its use in the early days, therefore, tended to be for ease of component construction, rather than as a weight-saving or strength-adding feature.

One major problem that would have prevented serious structural use of these early materials was that two-component, cold-set polyesters tended to suffer from instability. In early laminate life, the structure tended to harden, but in later years would then start to soften. Evidence of these changes can be seen in the cobweb-like cracking evident on early glass-reinforced-plastic car bodies. Competition vehicles tend not to be life dependent and therefore this instability did not concern constructors for use in non-structural components.

Over the years, the use of GRP extended enormously into a large number of industries and applications. This wide use had a considerable technical roll-on effect, resulting in improvements in the resin systems and a much larger selection of glass weaves and weights.

Although a wide range of production cars and boats, etc, utilized GRP, the attitude for the competition vehicle, with its ever-present weight concerns, was rather more conservative, but evidence of the ease of application and cheapness of GRP began to show in its growing use for competition-car bodywork.

The advent of aluminium honeycomb

Technology took a major step forward in 1938 when a patent was filed in England by Dr De Bruyne, in conjunction with the De Havilland Aircraft Company, on a material that was to have a far-reaching effect on the design of competition cars and motorcycles. This material was called honeycomb, and its function was as a structural-sandwich core material.

Although the patent was filed in 1938, honeycomb was not put into production in England until 1954. It is interesting to note that at the time of the early development of this material in England, a similar claim was being made in the USA, and to this day the 'who was first' question has never been positively answered.

All the early development of honeycomb was with aluminium. The method of construction during the development and early production years consisted of running aluminium foil through corrugated rollers to form corrugated sheets. An adhesive was then applied to raised portions of the corrugations, the sheets being stacked to produce a large block of hexagon-celled honeycomb. This block was then heat cured under light pressure, and glass rods were placed through the cells to prevent slippage during the curing process. The block was next cut into panels, or slices, to produce core material of the required thickness. How this core material was utilized is described later.

The need to produce larger panels than were possible with the corrugated method of making honeycomb, coupled with the ability to utilize high-performance adhesives for the node bond (the node being the adhesive join between the cells), led to the development of producing honeycomb by the expansion method.

This new method consists of printing lines of adhesive across the width of the roll of aluminium foil. This roll is then cut into sheets, which are stacked with the printed glue lines staggered (the number of sheets determines the length of the finished panel). This stack is then cured in a heated press under high pressure, resulting in what appears to be a solid block of aluminium.

The required honeycomb-panel thickness is achieved by machining a slice of the required thickness from the edge of the cured block. This slice is then expanded by tension, the unbonded areas parting to form the hexagon cells of the honeycomb.

Both this later method and the earlier corrugated method allow for variations in the mechanical properties of the honeycomb. These variations are possible by altering the cell size, and the thickness of the aluminium

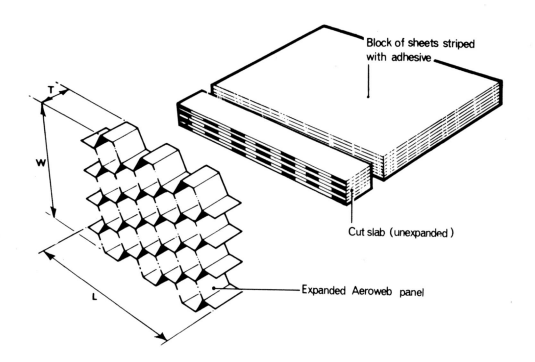

Block of sheets striped with adhesive

T

W

Cut slab (unexpanded)

L

Expanded Aeroweb panel

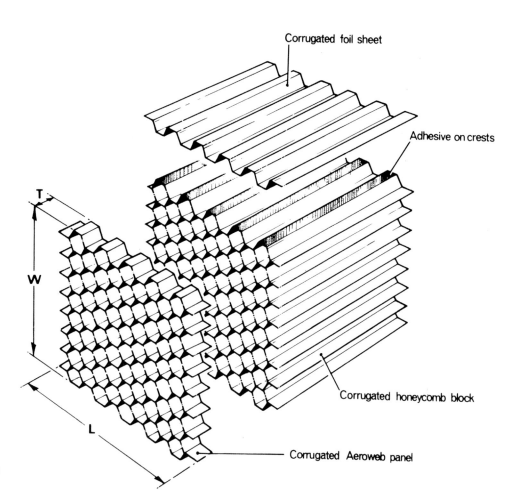

Corrugated foil sheet

Adhesive on crests

T

W

Corrugated honeycomb block

L

Corrugated Aeroweb panel

The two main methods of honeycomb manufacture: either flat sheets are glued together and then expanded to form the honeycomb, or ready-corrugated sheets are glued to make a honeycomb block. Sheets of the required thickness can then be cut from the block foil used, which means that material density can be controlled by foil thickness for a fixed cell size, but the ability to be able to select cell size means there are many permutations of properties.

The reasons for honeycomb having these various property potentials is to allow the designer to select the material best suited to the application.

Core density has a major effect on the compressive strength of a component, but with regard to component stiffness, the core thickness, coupled with the skin material, is a prime consideration, although density will also have some effect on stiffness.

There are components requiring both stiffness and compressive strength. Some may have a weight critical factor, but have areas requiring localized increased compressive strength. A designer will utilize the versatility of honeycomb performance to select the type most suitable for the application. Some components may have more than one type of honeycomb, as already mentioned, where weight is critical, but where there are localized high-compressive areas. How and where honeycomb is utilized in competition cars and motorcycles are described in the various case histories.

Wood as a chassis material

The first example of a composite competition-car structure known to the author was the wooden chassis of a famous hillclimb car called *Bloody Mary*, which was designed, built and driven by the legendary John Bolster. This was purely a home-built, one-off car, constructed around 1928–29, which utilized wooden beams as chassis side members.

Early home-built cars tended to be built and raced, being modified as necessary, and there appears, therefore, to be no documented test or performance data available. There is also no written evidence as to the reason for the use of the composite wood and steel construction. It is assumed that in this case, and in any other cases where wood has been used as a chassis material, it is due to its convenience to the home-builder rather than for technical or performance reasons.

2 Phenolic- and epoxy-resin systems

Phenolic-resin systems

GRP, having become a widely-used system, led to great advances in resin and, later on, fibre technology, some of this research having been started years before.

In addition to the polyester-resin systems, early research into phenolic-resin systems was utilized to produce a range of adhesives capable of bonding metal to metal to a high-enough standard to be widely used in aircraft construction, and utilized in the first known major composite competition-car project. This project is detailed in the series of case histories later in the book.

One major change was to take place with the advent of the phenolic adhesive; this was in curing. All previous GRP work had been carried out by two-part cold curing, and the cure was by chemical reaction; the new systems were thermo setting, or hot cured. This change to hot curing ensured better polymer cross-linking, and therefore a more stable resin layer, or adhesive, was produced. The new stability meant that the cured resin did not undergo physical changes, such as hardening and softening with time. Another significant gain was improved resistance to the atmosphere and to a wide range of chemicals.

At first, the new phenolic-based adhesives were supplied as a liquid-and-powder system, utilized by applying the liquid to the area to be bonded and then dusting on the coarse granular powder. Any excess powder was tipped off. The amount of powder retained by the liquid produced a mixture with the correct ratio of powder to liquid. This ratio could be controlled by supplying the powder with the correct granular size. A short open time, to allow residual solvents to evaporate from the liquid, was followed by a cure at elevated temperature and under pressure.

Cure temperature varied, according to supplier, but with early phenolics this would be in the region of 150 degrees Celsius under a pressure of 25–50 psi.

Although the new phenolic-based adhesives were supplied as a liquid and powder, they should not be confused with two-component adhesives, which cure by chemical reaction between the two components. In the case of phenolics, the liquid and powder would not cure when mixed until heat and pressure were applied.

The success of these phenolic systems soon led to the same formulations of powder and liquid being combined and formed into sheet or film form. Processing these new film-type adhesives was the same as for the separate liquid and powder, but handling became much easier and cleaner.

The film adhesive was supplied with a protective plastic backing, allowing it to be cut, by hand or punch, to the shape required. The advantages were that the adhesive could be applied accurately and where required. Of greater importance was the fact that the thickness of glue was always constant at the point of application.

Phenolic-adhesive systems did have some shortcomings, however. The maximum operating temperature tended to be low, in the region of 70 degrees Celsius, although in the early days this was not considered because these were the first structural adhesives and, therefore, somewhat sensational.

Another drawback was the production of volatiles during curing. Although these were mainly water vapour, they did necessitate the use of fairly high bonding pressures, which could be a problem with light and fragile components. Later, when these adhesives were used for bonding skins on to honeycomb to form sandwich structures, the honeycomb had to have small perforations in the cell walls to prevent the water vapour pressurizing the cells during the cure. These perforations were undesirable because if they allowed vapours out, they also allowed vapours in, making the honeycomb structure susceptible to environmental attack.

Specific requirements and further development led to modifications over the following years. Variants were produced with much improved maximum operating temperatures, but this was usually at the expense of some other feature, such as peel or shear strength. As a result, a variety of types was available, each having its own special feature. A large and complex structure, therefore, could utilize several different variants of a basic phenolic-resin system.

Phenolic adhesives are still used in very special applications but, in the main, epoxy-resin systems form the basis for the major part of bonding in structural applications. However, this valuable phenolic technology, although pushed aside by the advent of the epoxy adhesives, is now being used in the development of other forms of composite materials for totally different applications. These materials, which are now in use outside the competition-car field, have caught the attention of the car designers and are being given serious consideration. No doubt they will play a major part in the future of composite construction used for competition cars. The materials that utilize phenolic resins, and their potential uses, are described later.

It is interesting to note that the phenolic-resin systems that are probably the beginning of a new generation of composites have gone full circle since their early days in the 1930s, and are now finding a new place for different reasons.

Epoxy-resin systems

The mid-1960s saw the introduction of epoxy-resin systems. Epoxies, as with phenolics, were introduced as adhesive systems, but their development was to have a major influence on the composites in use today, as will be illustrated later in the description of modern composite systems used in the construction of competition cars and motorcycles.

Epoxy-resin systems were also thermo setting, or hot cured, but, as with the early polyesters, were available as two-part, cold-curing systems too. Although for fibre pre-impregnation, the system is usually thermo setting, or hot cured, and therefore a single-part resin system.

These systems have contributed a great deal to modern composites, for several reasons, and continue to do so.

In the main, epoxy resins are simple to use, both from the production of the pre-preg and the user's point of view. One major factor is that they lend themselves to modification in many ways, which has led to the availability of a very wide range of pre-preg types, each of which is tailored to perform in a certain manner.

Some pre-pregs will be adhesive; that is they are designed to laminate a skin on to a core material, such as honeycomb, in one shot or operation, to form a sandwich construction. Others will be laminating systems, designed for producing multi-layer laminates without the use of a core material.

In the case of laminates with a high number of layers or fibres, the resin is modified to prevent an exotherm taking place; that is the cure going out of control, resulting in a reaction that generates excessive temperatures. Exotherms can range from temperature rises just above the highest recommended cure temperature, giving a laminate of normal appearance but inferior performance, to temperatures high enough to cause total destruction of the laminate.

Other modifications include improvements in the laminate hot strength. In this case, the structure or component will retain a higher percentage of its structural performance at a higher temperature than a normal laminate. To achieve this higher temperature performance means using a higher cure temperature, in most cases, and an extended cure time. Or, as in some cases, the component may be subjected to a post cure; that is exposed to a further heat cycle, usually at a higher temperature than the first cure.

The most widely-used epoxy systems have cure temperatures in the region of 120 degrees Celsius. There are some systems that cure below 100 degrees Celsius, but due to their different curing reaction, these systems have a very limited shelf life, even when stored at sub-zero temperatures. At room temperature, their shelf life would be measured in days. The normal 120 degrees Celsius systems have a shelf life ranging from six months to a year at sub-zero temperatures, with a bench life of one to six months.

There will be exceptions to the pre-preg details outlined in most areas mentioned. These exceptions will usually be pre-pregs designed or modified for a specific purpose or experimentation. There will also be pre-pregs with differing resin systems, and the details will almost certainly be at variance with the descriptions given here, which are intentionally broad and only intended as a basic guide.

3 Fibre technology

Resin pre-impregnation

Another major advance in composite technology occurred in 1970. In fact, this step was so significant that the use of modern composites in competition cars and motorcycles is almost dependent on it. The advance was the introduction of the pre-impregnation of fibres with resin. This was made possible by the availability of thermo-setting, or hot-cured, resin systems.

Thermo-setting, or hot-cured, resin systems lend themselves to being cast as a film (as in film adhesive) or impregnated into fibres by heating to melting point. The melting-point temperature is controlled so as not to impose on the cure temperature, and during the resin's fluid state it is impregnated into the selected fibre by various mechanical means. Then, it is allowed to cool, resulting in a resin-filled fibre. In some cases, the resin may be fluidized by the addition of solvents, which are then evaporated off to leave the same resin-impregnated fibres. The resultant pre-impregnated fibres will now be in a flexible, but dry, state and are supplied in this form.

If the material is subjected to elevated temperatures up to, and beyond, its melting point, the resin content melts again. Increased temperature then affects the polymer cross-linking, or cure, and, after cooling, this gives a rigid resin-and-fibre mixture that will not fluidize again when heated.

The immediate advantages of the pre-impregnation of fibres are obvious. The resin-to-fibre ratio can be controlled very accurately, and the thickness of the impregnated fibres will be constant, as will the weight of the impregnated fibres. As will be seen, these are all aids to the designer when utilizing these materials. Adding to the versatility of the materials is the ability to select the required fibre range, which means fibre style, fibre weight and thickness, and, very important, type of weave.

The importance of the weave is illustrated by the fact that with all the available fibres, the maximum performance is achieved with the fibres in the straight mode, as with the tensile or compressive strength of a tube. If a tube of any material, be it paper or steel, is compressed by end loading, the maximum compressive strength is recorded when the tube is straight. This also applies with a tensile load, each end being pulled in tension. Therefore, the basic aim is to keep the distortion of the fibre to a minimum in any component. That is why, later in the development of pre-preg technology, UD (uni-directional) pre-pregs became available.

Uni-directional pre-pregs consist of totally unwoven fibres impregnated with resin. Early UD fibres, however, did have a cross-stitch of some other thread which was purely to hold the other structural fibres together during use. Further development led to UD pre-pregs being manufactured without the cross-stitch, enabling the constructor to achieve the maximum performance from any selected fibre, with a perfect appearance.

This type of pre-preg gives the designer the opportunity of utilizing the selected fibre's maximum performance, provided the component is of a shape, or configuration, that is suitable. When a component is of a shape that would cause undue distortion of the fibres of UD pre-preg, woven fibres would be substituted.

Pre-preg technology has led to a wide range of weave types being available, each having a reason for its selection, and these are all linked to the point about fibre distortion. This occurs when the fibres are separated or contorted by being utilized on compound curves or extremely complicated shapes. The various weave types are designed to optimize the fibre performance when used on these complicated shapes, and this is where the term 'drapability' applies.

Weave types known as satin weave and crowsfoot are designed to have good drapability; that is they can be formed into complicated shapes with the minimum of fibre distortion, bearing in mind that some distortion will have taken place in the weaving process.

The modern designer, therefore, has to consider the component to be made, from both aspects of performance and ease of construction. The many available weave types aid this selection, each one having its particular advantages. To extend the range further, in addition to the types of weave, there are many differing weights and thicknesses, increasing the versatility of pre-pregs.

The aim of selecting the correct pre-preg is to achieve the desired component performance with the minimum of construction difficulties; that means not using a plain weave style on a complicated shape, or a very drapable weave style on a simple shape. Performance requirements can be achieved, in the case of the more flexible pre-pregs, by the use of additional material. In some cases, however, this does cause a slight weight penalty.

Matrix resins

Pre-pregs are not just about weave types, but matrix resins as well. There are many, varied forms of epoxy resin, each having its own particular advantage. Some will have built-in toughness to give the finished component stiffness and good impact performance. To achieve this, some other less-desirable qualities manifest themselves, such as restricted flow, and this could affect the surface finish.

Other resin systems will be modified to give good high-temperature performance, some will be laminating pre-pregs (that is, for multi-layer laminates), and yet others will be adhesive pre-pregs, used for laminating skins on to a core material to form a sandwich structure. The range of pre-preg qualities is very wide, with differing weaves, resins for particular performances, weight, thickness, cure cycle and other technical aspects.

Carbon fibre and Kevlar

The scope for the designer was extended considerably in the late 1970s by the introduction of carbon fibre.

Carbon fibre is now offered in as wide a range of weave types, weights and thicknesses as was glass fibre before it. Coupled with the available resin systems, it enhances the potential of composites in structural applications.

Another fibre to follow carbon was Kevlar. This is an Aramid fibre with some special qualities, a brief description of which follows later. Kevlar, like the carbon and glass fibres, is woven and pre-impregnated with the same resin systems.

Phenolic-resin systems can be impregnated into the woven fibres, as with the epoxies, but phenolics do not have the right mechanical properties for the construction of competition cars and motorcycles. They could, however, find a place with advancing technology in the area covered by this book. The special qualities, and their potential use in these areas, are described later.

Fibre qualities

The fibres most widely used in the construction of competition vehicles are glass, carbon and Kevlar. All are pre-impregnated with a wide range of resin systems, and the choice of pre-preg for any given application will depend on two main points: performance and cost.

The performance aspect of the pre-preg will be dependent on requirement; that is stiffness, weight saving, impact resistance, or combinations of these qualities. The mechanical performance of the fibre dictates its selection, and in many cases, a combination of fibre types will be used in one component.

The mechanical performance figures, for what would be considered a standard range for each fibre form, are as follows:

	Carbon	Kevlar	Glass
Specific modulus	133.3	89.65	28.34
Specific strength	1722	2027	1387
Density G/cc	1.80	1.45	2.54

The above figures are arrived at by the method below:

$$\frac{\text{Modulus(GPA)}}{\text{Relative density}} \qquad \frac{\text{Tensile strength (MPa)}}{\text{Relative density}}$$

Due to the widely differing mechanical performance of the available fibres, the choice of fibre to save weight is not automatic. As can be seen, the lightest fibre does not have the best mechanical performance for the same structural use.

The performance figures quoted are for a comparison guide to the three most widely used fibres. There are variants of these fibres, and the variants will have differing performances, i.e. higher modulus or specific strength. These variants extend the choice of material for very specific areas of design, but other factors may have to be taken into account. Very high modulus carbon fibre, for instance, could enhance the stiffness of a component by a considerable amount, but would produce a part of a more brittle nature with reduced crack-stopping properties. The choice of materials, therefore, is made to suit the requirement from the finished component.

Many components will have more than one fibre type in the same structure, provided the resin types are compatible. The reasons for combining fibre types are varied. Some carbon components, body panels for example, may have carbon for stiffness and low weight, but a Kevlar layer to act as a fail-safe. The reason is that if the car body was fractured by impact, the brittle nature of the carbon would cause the laminate to break up, but the Kevlar would not break up in the same way. It would also serve to hold the fractured parts together.

The physical nature of Kevlar also gives a structure much better penetration resistance. This point is well illustrated by the wide use of Kevlar as a ballistic-protection material; that is bulletproof clothing and other ballistic armour.

Cost is another prime reason for fibre choice when the ultimate performance, or other technical reasons, are secondary. Pre-impregnated glass fibre costs approximately a fifth of the price of a similar weave and thickness of carbon, and a quarter of that of Kevlar, but in many cases it will have a structural performance sufficient for the component. The finished part would be heavier and be less stiff than in either carbon or Kevlar, but could be made to have sufficient stiffness by the use of extra material, if cost was more important than weight.

Glass laminates do not suffer from the same brittle nature as carbon laminates, so Kevlar is seldom used in conjunction with glass as a fail-safe, and as glass is the heaviest of the three fibre types, its use would indicate that the component is not weight sensitive. This is another reason for not using Kevlar with glass. Also, since glass is by far the cheapest of the three fibre types, it will technically be suitable for a wide range of components where cost is more important than ultimate performance.

For components where weight saving is more important than ultimate structural performance, i.e. body panels, fairings, ducting etc, Kevlar may be used, as it is the lightest of the described fibres and lends itself to maximum weight savings using currently-available materials.

Where components, in the main, utilize glass or Kevlar, carbon fibre is often used in specific areas to provide local stiffening or strength. For example, on bodywork or fairings, return flanges may be strengthened by the localized use of carbon. On large panels, or where there is little shape to assist stiffness, carbon can again be used in specific areas to achieve the required stiffness. It will be noted from the quoted figures that Kevlar has the highest specific strength and a fairly high specific modulus. From a stiffness point of view, it can be inferior to carbon, but superior to glass. However, it does tend to suffer from interlaminar shear failure; that is separation of the laminate layers. This phenomenon is due to Kevlar being weaker in compression; that is end loading on the fibre.

Kevlar's lower strength in compression is due to the physical structure of the fibre itself. Both carbon and glass are homogenous, or solid, fibres, but Kevlar has many tiny fibrils, or microscopic fibres, within each individual fibre.

If a fibre is bent, the surface of the fibre on the outside of the bend is in tension, and the surface on the inside of the bend is in compression. The homogenous, or solid, nature of carbon and glass, therefore, resists both tension and compression forces to the limit of the fibre material itself. In the case of Kevlar, the fibre surface on the outside of the bend resists the tensile load, but the compressive loads on the inside cause the tiny fibrils within the main fibre to separate and buckle. This compressive breakdown is the probable cause of Kevlar laminates being susceptible to interlaminar shear failure.

As mentioned previously, Kevlar has excellent penetration resistance. This is due to the physical nature of the fibre. When a Kevlar laminate is hit by a missile, penetration is resisted by the separation of the tiny fibrils within each single fibre. This separation absorbs the energy of the missile, and the same principle applies when attempts are made to tear or cut Kevlar. This quality of resistance makes Kevlar ideal for use as a fail-safe layer in a laminate.

There will be many variants of the individual fibres and differences in their performance. In some areas, very-high-performance glass, for example, may approach the performance of the lower grades of carbon, but it will always be heavier. Consequently, the main qualities of the three fibre types will always dictate their selection to meet a specific requirement.

4 Process methods

When utilizing modern composites, the process methods will vary for several reasons: type of component, type of composite needed for the particular component, available equipment, and also the performance and finish required from the component. The first consideration will be the shape, or configuration, of the component. From this point of view, the main criterion is whether the component is flat or contoured.

Flat components utilizing a core material to form a sandwich structure (this could be aluminium skins on a core material, or a multi-layer laminate on its own) can be processed with a platen press or on a surface table under vacuum, both of which apply the required pressure. This type of flat panel could be constructed using cold-set resin systems, but structures of the type covered by this book will, in the main, be thermo setting, or hot cured. Therefore, in these cases, the equipment must be capable of being heated or withstanding temperatures consistent with the required cure cycle.

If a press is used, both top and bottom platens will be heated by some method: steam, electricity or hot oil. Pressure is usually applied by controlled hydraulics.

Surface tables may be heated by the same methods as for a press, but as the pressure for the bond, or consolidation, is by vacuum, this means that the component is heated from one side only. Therefore, unless the component is very thin, another heat source is required to ensure a correct and even cure temperature. This usually takes the form of an oven.

When contoured, or shaped, components are to be made, the use of the vacuum-bag method is almost exclusive. There are some cases where special two-piece tooling (that is a top and bottom mould) can be designed for use in a press, but in almost all the areas covered by this book, a single-sided mould and vacuum bag are utilized. (This method does require an independent heat source, such as an oven or an autoclave.)

The autoclave is a pressure vessel capable of being heated over the required range. The advantage of using an autoclave is its ability to achieve much higher bonding pressures. Vacuum curing, although suitable as a method in almost all cases, does limit the workpiece to only one atmosphere pressure during the cure, which is approximately 14 psi. The autoclave can be pressurized to give bonding pressures of 100 psi and more.

The higher pressure during the resin cure cycle serves to ensure total consolidation of a laminate, considered essential, in some cases, to eliminate voids. It also serves to ensure that all the component parts, or laminate layers, are completely pressed into place in the mould, particularly in complicated and large components.

The material configuration for a pre-made flat honeycomb panel
1 Top facing skin
2 Film adhesive
3 Honeycomb core
4 Bottom facing skin
5 Film adhesive

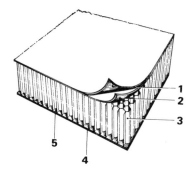

Two examples of steam-heated presses used to produce flat sandwich panels from composite materials

Tooling and moulds

To produce a component of any type or shape in modern composites, some form of tooling or mould is required. In the case of flat panels, where aluminium skins are being bonded on to a core material, or a laminated pre-preg skin is used, the press platens themselves act as the tooling; where pre-pregs are being utilized, a caul plate may be used. The latter is a thin sheet material, such as aluminium, which is placed between the component and press platen and serves as an aid to achieving a good component finish.

When laminated pre-pregs form the skin material, the selected number of layers may be placed on the core, press cured to form the laminate, and bonded on to the core in one operation. However, in some special cases, the layers of pre-preg may be press cured, or cured by some other method, such as vacuum or autoclave, into a fully-cured and consolidated laminate, which is then bonded to the core material with a hot-cured film adhesive. This method of pre-consolidating the skins is normally employed when uni-directional pre-pregs are being used. It keeps distortion of the fibre to a minimum and, therefore, ensures the maximum performance from that pre-preg.

Presses for this type of panel production require considerable capital expenditure and have limited use in the areas covered by this book. The comparatively small amount of flat panel work found in competition cars and motorcycles is usually subcontracted to one of the many bonding shops specializing in this type of production.

When the component is contoured, or shaped (such as bodywork, one-piece chassis, ducting etc), some form of mould tool is required. The first consideration is for male or female tooling. The deciding factors are ease of lay-up, that is the tailoring of the selected materials into the tool or mould prior to cure, and the required finish to the component, bearing in mind that, in satisfying these points, the finished component must meet the design requirements from a structural point of view.

Before making the mould tool, male or female, a master shape must be produced, as previously described for wet lay-up moulds. The basic principle for making the moulds is very similar to that used for moulds for wet lay-up, except that as the materials to be moulded are thermo-setting, or hot-cured, pre-pregs, the resin system must be of a type capable of withstanding working temperatures in excess of the cure temperatures of the pre-pregs to be used.

Polyester has been the most widely-used mould-making resin for many years, but the earlier versions would not tolerate the common cure temperatures that were in excess of 100 degrees Celsius. Epoxy tooling resins filled this gap, being capable of surviving repeated exposure to cure cycles of over 100 degrees Celsius, but they were much more expensive and took longer to produce the required mould.

Eventually, polyester-resin technology met the need and progressed to making available polyesters that were capable of withstanding repeated 120-degree Celsius cures, and were cheaper and simpler to use than the epoxy systems. This resulted in the widespread use of polyester moulds for pre-preg tooling.

Pre-preg technology has progressed, leading to the introduction of pre-pregs with much higher TG, that is Glass Transition, resulting in finished components with much higher service temperatures. (These may be necessary in areas of localized high-temperature exposure.) This type of high-temperature pre-preg will usually have a much higher cure temperature, in the region of 175 degrees Celsius, and in many cases much extended cure times (sometimes several hours). In turn, this can be followed by a post cure (again, this could be for several hours) at even higher temperatures of up to 240 degrees Celsius or more. These higher-temperature-curing pre-pregs demand much more from the tooling resins which, in most cases, will again be high-performance epoxy systems.

The woven fabric type to be used, in conjunction with the selected resin system, is important to the finished tooling. Although many carbon-fibre components are manufactured in glass-fibre-based tooling, it is usual for major components, such as chassis, or components with close finished tolerances to utilize tooling fabrics of a similar type to those used to make the component itself. In other words, glass pre-pregs will utilize glass-based tooling, and carbon pre-pregs, carbon-based tools. This is to accommodate the coefficient of expansion of both pre-preg and tooling. In many cases, technical reasons may dictate the choice of tooling materials, but for secondary structures, cost may be the deciding factor.

The actual construction of the tooling mould, by the wet lay-up method, will be the same as for moulds for wet lay-up components, except for the selection of a suitable resin system.

Technology on the tooling side has progressed to the use of pre-pregs as mould-making materials, but this does add to the tooling cost. This is due to the tooling pre-pregs being more expensive than wet lay-up materials, and because the resultant mould made with pre-preg materials requires heat curing and, in practice, takes longer to make. However, tooling or moulds made by the use of pre-pregs are claimed to be stronger and more durable which, in some cases, may justify the additional cost.

When the resin-and-fibre mould tool, in whatever form, is complete, it must undergo a post-curing operation, i.e. the mould is subjected to a cycle time and temperature similar to the pre-preg to be used in the mould. Under ideal conditions, this post-cure process may be carried out several times prior to use.

The final stage, prior to lay-up of the component, is the releasing of the mould; that is surface pre-treatment to prevent the component from sticking in the mould. There are many methods and many release agents available, but care must be exercised in their selection. For example, the release agent for an aluminium mould may not be suitable for a resin-based mould, but some release agents are claimed to be suitable for all types of moulds. Suppliers of composite materials are always ready to advise on the best type of release agent for the materials to be used.

Some composite manufacturing facilities insist on the mould being waxed prior to application of the release agent. Others claim that this is not necessary. The insistance on using wax could be a legacy from the days when moulds were made for wet lay-up, when wax was, in many cases, the only release agent available.

The mould should now be ready for use, and different constructors will approach the lay-up of a component in different ways, but basic methods will follow similar lines.

Lay-up

Prior to cutting the pre-preg, it is usual practice to prepare templates. This is normally done by using thin paper, which is cut and trimmed to fit the part or total mould area to be covered by laminate. These templates, or patterns, may be in as many pieces as necessary to accommodate the complexity of the mould or component shape. When the component is to be produced in numbers, the templates are usually cut from some form of more durable material, such as thin aluminium, stiff card etc.

The complexity of shape, structural or aesthetic considerations, and personal choice are all points that need consideration when planning or carrying out the component lay-up procedure. An example of lay-up procedure is given below, taking as a basis a hypothetical body panel.

A panel of this type will utilize a single-sided female mould, and will be cured under vacuum. The pre-cut pre-preg shapes will be laid into the mould, then stretched and pressed to cover the mould surface. Some pre-pregs will be tacky and, therefore, easy to stick in place. Others, that are drier, may be stuck in place by the use of a hand-held hot-air blower, rather like an industrial version of a hair drier.

The use of hot-air blowers is common practice, as they serve not only to stick the pre-preg in place, but also to lower the viscosity of, or soften, the resin, which allows the woven fibres of the pre-preg to move within the weave. This makes the pre-preg more drapable, which assists in forming it into and around complex shapes.

The number of pre-preg layers required will be dependent on several factors: component stiffness, impact resistance, minimum weight, and whether the component is to be a multi-layer laminate or a honeycomb-sandwich structure. The type of fibre and pre-preg thickness add to the versatility of this type of construction.

During the first stages of lay-up, after the first layer has been placed in the mould, consideration is given to special areas, i.e. return or edge flanges, areas requiring extra strength, or inserts and attachment points. These special areas can be stiffened, strengthened or thickened by the addition of extra layers of pre-preg or, where the main material is glass pre-preg, the additional strength may be provided by the use of carbon-fibre pre-preg. The latter will give additional strength with a minimum of extra weight.

Once the special areas have been attended to, the remaining layers of pre-preg are placed in the mould until the required thickness is achieved. This will change during the cure, but all pre-preg suppliers will state a finished thickness that can be expected from the selected type or types of pre-preg. Where honeycomb sandwich is to be utilized, the pre-preg will be of the adhesive type and, therefore, should require no further preparation.

In most cases where honeycomb is used in body panels, and particularly with complex shapes, non-metallic honeycomb, such as Nomex, will be selected. Honeycomb made from Nomex, and at a low density, will be far more drapable than metallic honeycomb, and will be far more resilient. Therefore, in the finished state, it is more suitable for this type of component.

The honeycomb is cut to shape and size, using paper templates or patterns, as for the pre-preg. Although the honeycomb can be tried and trimmed before finally placing it in the mould, the resin-rich pre-preg necessary for sandwich construction will hold it in place, with the assistance of a hot-air blower.

At this stage of the lay-up there is a very important step to be taken, and that is to use a foaming resin system to join the honeycomb together where, for ease of construction or some technical reason, it has been put in place in several pieces. Such foaming resin systems come in thick-film or paste form. Both serve the same purpose, ease of use or personal choice being the usual deciding factors between them.

The function of the foaming resin is to expand at the cure stage and join the sections of honeycomb together to give structural continuity. It is also used when inserts or hard parts are to be included in the lay-up. Again, the foam gives continuity between insert, or hard point, and the rest of the structure, distributing point loads into the component. In addition, foam is placed around the outer edge of the honeycomb as a fillet, or filler, where the pre-preg back skin folds over to seal the honeycomb into the structure.

With outer skin, honeycomb and inserts in place, the final stage of component lay-up is the addition of the inner pre-preg skin. This is laid over the materials in the mould. The hot-air blower can again be used to plasticize the pre-preg to improve drapability and to hold it in place. The required number of pre-preg layers are applied, as for the outer skin. In theory, a laminated pre-preg honeycomb-sandwich component should be balanced; that is the skins on each side of the sandwich should be of the same material and equal thickness. This prevents thermal stress during the resin cure.

In the case of flat, or almost flat, panels and components, the theory of balanced laminates is important, but in the case of shaped components, such as body panels, it is common for the inner skin to be thinner. This saves weight and material. The stiffness of sandwich structures, coupled with complex shape, is sufficient to resist undue distortion.

The lay-up description given is only intended as a basic guide, as each case or component will require special considerations and actions, such as the application of strips of pre-preg at joggles or steps in the mould surface. These ease the path of the pre-preg around the sudden changes in the mould surface by filling the step, and also ensure a resin-rich and, therefore, good surface finish at a critical point. Some constructors do not utilize this practice of inserting additional pre-preg strips, but make a concerted effort to tailor the pre-preg into these difficult corners with a hot-air blower and some form of spatula.

The lay-up principles for modern composite components will be similar, whatever their size or shape. This also applies for the range of fibres, and whether the component is a multi-layer laminate or sandwich structure. As with other materials and processes, the use of composites develops the technician's skill, and each individual will find materials, methods of use, and many other points that will help achieve a finished component of the required standard.

Final preparation and cure cycle

The hypothetical panel is now ready for final preparation prior to the cure cycle. This is to put the component under vacuum. The procedure will follow similar lines, whether the cure is to be under vacuum only or in an autoclave under pressure.

Vacuum only means that the cure takes place at atmospheric pressure. This method is the most widely used where cost is important. The oven required for this type of cure costs a fraction of the price of an autoclave, and is also cheaper to operate.

Atmospheric pressure is normally considered adequate for a wide range of components, such as bodywork, fairings, ducting etc. However, the autoclave receives serious consideration for structural components, such as chassis, or multi-layer laminates which, like chassis, require total consolidation of the pre-preg layers to achieve the ultimate performance from the selected material. For purpose of example, the cure for the hypothetical body panel will be by vacuum.

Following completion of the lay-up, the next stage is to cover the entire pre-preg area with a release film. This is normally a thin, very flexible plastic film, the purpose of which is to prevent the pre-preg resin sticking to other covering materials. It also serves to give the component a clean, finished surface on the inner face. In many cases, this release film will have very tiny perforations, the theory being that they allow a free passage for the air being sucked out and prevent vacuum cut-off. However, some users claim them to be unnecessary. They are, therefore, one of the many permutations of available materials to satisfy the constructor's preference or need.

The next stage is to cover the entire area of the component with an air-bleed mat. Again, this comes in various forms, some resembling a very-low-density, temperature-resistant foam, others having the appearance of a very loose, soft, felt-type material. The purpose of this layer is twofold: to ensure a free passage for the extracted air, and to give protection to the vacuum bag by cushioning all protrusions.

The final pre-cure stage is to fit the vacuum bag, which can be tailor-made in silicone rubber suitable for repeated use, or be formed from disposable temperature-resistant plastic sheet.

The silicone-rubber bag is moulded to follow the contours of the component shape and, in use, is sealed to the periphery of the mould, usually by some form of clamping. This method is expensive for use on small runs, but is used when the component is to be produced in large numbers.

The second, and most widely used, method in the area covered by this book is the use of the disposable vacuum bag. In most cases, the material is a nylon derivative, but trade names do not necessarily indicate chemical composition. Whatever the material source, the method is the same.

A land, or flange, will have been allowed for around the periphery of the mould during its construction. This flange serves to hold a bead of sealing material, usually in the form of a tacky, paper-backed extrusion.

The plastic vacuum-bag material is then laid over the entire lay-up and is held in place by the adhesive sealing material stuck to the outer mould flange. The bag must be slack to allow it to be sucked into all the shapes and tight corners.

In most cases, the vacuum bag will be formed from a flat sheet and must be tailored to a complex shape. This will lead to many unavoidable folds and overlaps. However, these are not a disadvantage; in fact, the folds are essential to ensure total freedom for the bag to form to the shape required, and prevent bridging, i.e. when the bag material spans a corner or a deep hollow. Where this occurs, the area underneath receives little, or no, pressure, resulting in a lack of consolidation and resin starvation.

To form the folds, it will be necessary to put tucks in the vacuum bag around the edge where it is held by the sealing tape. These tucks are produced by using short lengths of sealing material in vertical columns running from the edge seal. The vacuum bag then makes a detour around the columns to produce folds, making more material available at these points. As many of these tucks as necessary can be put in to give the bag freedom of movement, or to use up excess material.

During the tailoring of the vacuum bag, temperature-recording thermocouples and vacuum take-off points will have been put in place. One of the take-off points will be used for a vacuum-gauge connection.

The take-off points can be simple, small-bore pipes sealed into the vacuum bag via the edge seal or, as more widely used, purpose-made valves. These can be put in any convenient place in the bag by cutting a hole, the valve clamping the bag material between two sealing surfaces. These valves have snap-on connectors and incorporate snap-off seals so that the vacuum is retained when the vacuum pipe is disconnected.

Once the component is under vacuum and there are no perceptible air leaks, the mould is taken through the cure cycle, and in the example case, a hot-air-circulating oven is utilized as the source of heat. This is a widely-used method.

The cure cycle (that is time, temperature and, in some cases, specified heat-up rate) will depend on the resin type and formulation. All this relevant processing information, and the process instructions, will be detailed in the supplier's data sheet. It is important that vacuum is retained throughout the cure and until the component has cooled to a safe temperature which, with most resin systems, is below 70 degrees Celsius.

In most cases, where glass pre-pregs are cured in glass-based tooling or moulds, the component is allowed to cool completely before it is removed from the mould, but where carbon components are made in glass-based moulds, it is advisable to remove the component from the mould as soon as it can be handled. This is because the mould expands during heat-up, and the carbon component forms at this stage to the expanded mould size.

Above Here is an example of a composite component with compound curves. It was formed from glass pre-preg over a honeycomb core, and cured in one shot under vacuum. The panel is part of a Formula One car's radiator duct

Right A sample pre-preg and honeycomb sandwich lay-up. In the background is the finished dish-shaped component, while the example on the left shows the mould with both inner and outer skins and honeycomb in place. On the right, a release film covers the lay-up. The woven glass air-bleed layer can also be seen and is covered by the vacuum sheet, which is secured with heat-resistant sealing strip

Right A typical carbon-fibre-skinned, honeycomb component of tapering thickness—one possible method of wing construction

Below Here are some examples of simple, pre-preg-skinned, honeycomb sandwich—a typical configuration that could be used for areas such as undertrays, side pods etc

However, due to carbon's extremely low coefficient of expansion, the component does not contract with the mould. This can result in the mould pinching the component, making removal difficult. When large components, such as chassis, are to be made in carbon fibre, the moulds are also made in this material to eliminate the problem. The use of carbon moulds also utilizes the material's low expansion rate to achieve close component tolerances.

The lay-up method described previously would also be used for an autoclave cure. Once under vacuum, the component would be placed in the autoclave and pressurized to the required bonding pressure. Cure temperature and time should be the same as for an oven cure, vacuum still being applied throughout.

In some cases, when an autoclave cure is being used, the component may have reduced or low vacuum, for there is a theory that when very thick, multi-layer laminates are being produced, positive pressure only ensures a void-free laminate. The other reason for maintaining a reduced vacuum is as an indicator of a bag leak during the cure. If positive pressure only was used and the bag sprung a leak, it would pressurize, resulting in no positive pressure on the component. A small indicated vacuum suddenly disappearing indicates a bag leak. If the applied vacuum is then increased to draw off the air leaking in the component, it remains under pressure and, therefore, is saved. Use of this low-vacuum technique requires close monitoring of the cure operation throughout.

Further refinements

Lay-up procedures will vary according to component configurations. For example, where multi-layer laminates are being made, particularly over an extreme component shape, the pre-preg may be consolidated into position by the use of a vacuum bag. After each, or every few layers, the same vacuum bag is utilized to effect the cure of the laminated component.

Some major components, utilizing honeycomb to form a sandwich structure, will be constructed as a two-stage cure. First, the outer pre-preg skin will be vacuumed down and fully cured on its own. This skin will be covered by a film adhesive for fixing the honeycomb in place, which is added to the lay-up next, together with the inner skin. The adhesive and the inner skin are then cured under vacuum, as a second and final stage. This two-stage process is used for two main reasons:

1 In a major component, such as a chassis, where there are many pre-preg layers, to ensure that the first is completely consolidated and meets requirements. (In other words, it serves as a check that all is as it should be prior to investing further time and materials.)

2 Surface finish. By applying a vacuum cure directly to a skin lay-up, total consolidation is ensured due to the atmospheric pressure being applied to the entire surface rather than just the areas in contact with the honeycomb cell ends.

The two-stage process does increase the cost, and many constructors

An example of an early
Formula One chassis
fabricated from pre-made flat
panels. The honeycomb
sandwich structure can be
clearly seen around the nose
and other apertures

consider it unnecessary, but it is another demonstration of the versatility of
composite technology.

Whatever the component configuration, large, small, solid laminate or
honeycomb sandwich, the basic principles for composite use will be similar.
They are that a mould or tool is required and is treated with a release agent,
pre-preg of the selected type is layered into place, and pressure is applied
and maintained throughout the supplier's recommended cure cycle.

The way in which the lay-up of the composite materials is approached
will depend on the operator's skill and preference. Both will vary from
person to person, each having his or her individual method or technique
of making the finished component to a required standard.

Many components are made from pre-made, flat, honeycomb-sandwich
boards. These boards can be made to meet a design requirement; that is
honeycomb type, density, cell size and thickness. The skin materials can be
selected to meet the requirement, either metallic or non-metallic. These flat
panels are usually made in heated platen presses, but can be produced under
vacuum in a standard oven or autoclave. The panel is laid up on a flat, rigid
base, and a second, thinner plate (a caul plate) is placed on top to give a
good finish on both sides. This lay-up is then placed under a vacuum bag,
as for a shaped component, and cured as previously described.

Flat panels can be cut to shape and a component fabricated from the cut
pieces. They can be bonded together with, if necessary, covering strips over
the joins to give skin continuity. Alternatively, extrusions of either internal
or external design can be used as a joining method or a fabricated positive
link between sections.

By far the most popular and cleverest method of utilizing flat panels to construct components is by what is known as the cut-and-fold method. This involves cutting through one skin with a router or saw which, in effect, weakens the sandwich structure at that point, and the panel will bend at the cut line until the edges meet. By calculation, the correct amount of skin can be removed to achieve any angle of bend required. Adhesive is applied to the exposed honeycomb cell ends, the bend is made and the panel restrained in that position until the adhesive has set. For structural applications, a covering strip of a similar material to the skin is bonded over the cut to restore skin continuity.

Very complex shaped components can be made using the cut-and-fold method. One way to consider the versatility of this technique is that if you can fold a model of the required component from stiff card, then the component itself can be made from honeycomb sandwich. This method has long been used for producing race-car chassis, and is still in use (as can be seen later in this book). It has also recently been extended to motorcycles.

Composites are very versatile from the material point of view, and this versatility is extended by the methods and techniques of their use. Each component will be manufactured to requirements by a method devised to be suitable to available equipment and skill.

This section of the book has given a basic description of methods of use of composites; the following sections will outline the history and describe the current use of composites in competition cars and motorcycles.

An early development of the non-metallic racing-car monocoque, constructed from pre-made flat panels and assembled using the cut-and-fold method. The skins are a mixture of carbon fibre and Kevlar, while the core material is Nomex honeycomb

Part Two   Composites in competition cars

1 Summary
2 Benetton Formula
3 Cooper
4 Ferrari
5 Ford UFO 2 Project
6 TWR Jaguar
7 Lola Cars
8 Team Lotus
9 McLaren
10 Motor Racing Developments (Brabham)
11 Reynard Racing
12 Williams GP Engineering

I Summary

There have been many interesting and varied users of modern composites since their availability for the construction of competition cars and motor-cycles, and it would be impossible to include details of them all. The case histories included in this book, however, are considered to have been major or significant steps in the use of composites, or illustrate trends among teams and manufacturers of current renown.

Among the many important designs utilizing composites is a sports car built in the 1960s by Chaparral in the USA. This car was significant because the chassis was made using wet lay-up GRP, and this was quite early in composite development for a car chassis to be structurally dependent on a resin-and-fibre mixture. Chaparral did race the car successfully in this form, but eventually reverted to an all-aluminium monocoque.

Another significant, early user of wet lay-up GRP was Lotus Cars. Their range of early sportscars utilized these materials in structural and non-structural areas. There is no detailed case history of this sportscar production, as they employed materials prior to those covered by this book.

The first notable event in the utilization of modern composites, as illustrated by the following case histories, was the structural use of honey-comb sandwich. Initially, its use was strategic, several well-known chassis designers incorporating the material in small quantities in areas such as fuel cells and side pods. Eventually, this led to the use of honeycomb sandwich as a structural monocoque or chassis material.

The first structural use of honeycomb sandwich was, without exception, made with aluminium skin bonded on to aluminium honeycomb, using hot-cured film adhesive. The resultant chassis designs, therefore, were fabricated from pre-made flat panels. Apart from the designs covered by the team case histories, there have been other notable cars that used this form of chassis design, built by teams that no longer operate. These include the Fittipaldi and Wolf. Although the latter did not boast an illustrious career, it was reputed to have had one of the best chassis of the period. Another team to utilize the aluminium-sandwich panel-and-fabrication method was Spirit. These, and others, were designer variations on what was becoming an almost standard range of materials and methods. The all-metal sandwich structure was to give way to the use of non-metallic material, although the change-over was not total. As can be seen from the case histories, this method of chassis fabrication is still retained and forms the basis of chassis design for cars that race in the CART series, where the bottom half of the monocoque, or chassis, has to be deformable.

Since the progression in chassis design to utilizing carbon and Kevlar as skin materials on honeycomb to form the sandwich structure, this basic form of construction has become universal in Formula One. However, as the case histories show, the basic form is arrived at by different methods and combinations of materials.

Apart from the teams detailed, there have been excellent chassis designs in this form from teams that have been winners and teams that have yet to win. Ligier, for example, is another leading contender in Formula One who again utilizes materials and methods similar to other Formula One manufacturers, resulting in cars that are technically advanced in the use of modern composites.

The Barclay Arrows are long-term campaigners in Formula One and, as well as other composite components on their cars, they have an excellent carbon-and-honeycomb monocoque. Although yet to come to the forefront, they have achieved some good places high in the field, marking a competitive and tenacious team.

One of the more recent Formula One teams to produce a car that is almost totally dependent on modern composites and which is, without a doubt, very advanced technically, is Team Haas, USA, Lola Ford. Their car has a carbon-skinned, honeycomb-sandwich-structure monocoque, made by similar methods to those described previously. This also goes for the remainder of the components on the car. It must be pointed out that this, and all other designs, achieve their individuality by the designer's selection and processing of the available composite materials.

The Team Haas car was the first to use the new Ford V6, and it is beginning to show its competitiveness. From the drawing board to its current state in only two years, it is a credit to its designers, Neil Oatley and John Baldwin, Carl Haas and all concerned with the team.

One important and world-renowned manufacturer, who has employed modern composites in a wide range of motor-racing vehicles, is March Engineering. This company is one of the world's largest commercial manufacturers to various sportscar specifications, including endurance types. Other formula types include CART or Indianapolis, Formula One, and various other single-seaters.

Most of the composite technology described throughout this book is being utilized, wherever the commercial aspect allows, by March Engineering. The list of race victories by cars from this manufacturer is almost endless, and their extensive, in-house composite facilities will ensure that modern composites continue to be the basis of many future winners. A lot of successful racers and competition-car owners waiting for success form a tribute to Robin Herd and those in his company.

The composite technology available in the UK has resulted in Roger Penske setting up his operation there to take full advantage of this fact in the preparation of his excellent and very successful CART or Indianapolis series cars. These follow similar construction lines as the previously-described CART cars; that is deformable chassis bottom half and composite top half, bodywork, undertrays, and side pods, all utilizing composite materials processed by the now standard methods. Little needs saying about the success enjoyed by cars from this team.

Teams that have built cars by methods and materials that are now the state of the art, but have yet to come to the forefront of Formula One, include Data General Team Tyrrell. This team has shown periods of great potential and has been in the fray for many seasons. Others utilizing composite technology, but who have yet to make their mark in this very competitive field, are West Zakspeed, Osella and Minardi.

Teams who no longer exist, but who produced excellent cars based on modern composites include Renault, who utilized composites to the full in producing an extremely competitive car which was a race winner for a considerable part of its existance. Most of its components were manufactured by methods already described here. Alfa Romeo was another well-known team to produce competitive Formula One cars based on modern composites; their competitive history is well known.

The ATS, although never a leading contender, was, at the time it raced, considered by many to have one of the best-made carbon chassis on the circuit. Ram was another team to utilize modern composites, but was unable to reach the top of this very competitive sport.

These current and past race-car constructors, in their effort to produce competitive cars, have enforced rapid progress in the use of modern composites. The knowledge thus gained by both composite suppliers and users will ensure that this and other industries will benefit to the full from this exciting technology.

Below One of the later composite-based Renault Formula One cars at speed

Right Eddie Cheever in one of the Renault Formula One cars that relied heavily on composite construction

Right This diagram of
Bluebird shows the positions
of the structural honeycomb
sandwich panels

Far right Film adhesive being
put in place during the
construction of panels for
Bluebird. Redux was used
over most areas, but Hedux
was employed in the vicinity
of the exhaust ducts

Below far right A 26 ft long
main beam at the lay-up
stage. The honeycomb is
clearly visible, as are the solid
metal inserts that serve as
attachment points for various
components. All were
bonded together in one
operation

Below Donald Campbell's
CN7 Bluebird during a trial
·run at Goodwood. The
record-breaking car was 30 ft
long, 8 ft wide, 4 ft 9 in. high
and weighed 4 tons. It was
powered by a Proteus gas
turbine engine and travelled
on special 52 in. diameter
Dunlop tyres. Braking was
provided by a combination of
Girling discs and air flaps at
each side

Record-breaking composites

The 1950s saw the design and construction of a competition car that was
to be structurally dependent on modern composites and, in this respect,
was ahead of its time. This very famous car was Donald Campbell's CN7
Bluebird. It was the Campbell Norris 7 project, designed by Norris Bros
for an attempt on the world land-speed record for cars with driven wheels;
at that time, the record was held by the late John Cobb at 394 mph.

The frame, or chassis, of Bluebird was novel in that its main beams,
auxiliary beams, engine covers, pressure bulkheads and canopy frame consisted of aluminium skins bonded on to Aeroweb aluminium honeycomb
with synthetic-resin adhesives, in film form, to produce structural sandwich
components. The layout of the main frame was an egg-box-type arrangement assembled from the sandwich-construction panels.

The chassis consisted of two main frames running lengthwise which, in
profile, were of a similar shape to the body outline. These main beams were
held apart by transverse bulkheads which formed bays to house the engine,
transmission and driver. The profile of these transverse bulkheads again
followed the shape of the body outline. This chassis design resulted in a
structure that met performance requirements and was of a suitable shape to
serve as a body frame; that is shaped alloy panels were tailored to fit directly
on to the chassis structure.

The design was remarkable because it was the first structure of this kind
to use honeycomb in a totally structural configuration and was solely
dependent on hot-cured film adhesives. What makes it even more remarkable was the fact that the main beams were 26 ft long and 3 ft deep.

Two types of adhesive were used in the construction; a Redux adhesive
was used in most areas, with Hidux being utilized in areas requiring a higher
temperature performance. Solid metal inserts were let into the honeycomb
and sandwiched between the skins to serve as attachment points or load-
bearing areas. All these inserts etc were put in place at the lay-up stage and
bonded in a steam-heated platen press.

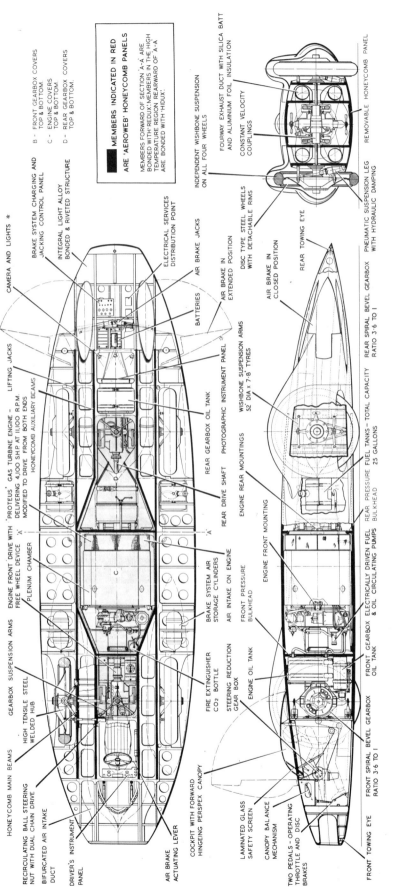

MEMBERS INDICATED IN RED ARE 'AEROWEB' HONEYCOMB PANELS

MEMBERS FORWARD OF SECTION 'A-A' ARE BONDED WITH REDUX: MEMBERS IN THE HIGH TEMPERATURE REGION REARWARD OF A-A ARE BONDED WITH 'HIDUX'.

B - FRONT GEARBOX COVERS TOP & BOTTOM
C - ENGINE COVERS TOP & BOTTOM
D - REAR GEARBOX COVERS TOP & BOTTOM.

HONEYCOMB MAIN BEAMS
RECIRCULATING BALL STEERING NUT WITH DUAL CHAIN DRIVE
BIFURCATED AIR INTAKE DUCT
DRIVER'S INSTRUMENT PANEL
AIR BRAKE ACTUATING LEVER
GEARBOX SUSPENSION ARMS
HIGH TENSILE STEEL WELDED HUB
COCKPIT WITH FORWARD HINGEING PERSPEX CANOPY
CANOPY BALANCE MECHANISM
LAMINATED GLASS SAFETY SCREEN
TWO PEDALS - OPERATING THROTTLE AND DISC BRAKES
FRONT TOWING EYE
FRONT SPIRAL BEVEL GEARBOX RATIO 3·6 TO 1
FRONT GEARBOX ELECTRICALLY DRIVEN FUEL & OIL CIRCULATING PUMPS
FRONT GEARBOX OIL TANK
ENGINE OIL TANK
STEERING REDUCTION GEAR BOX
FIRE EXTINGUISHER CO2 BOTTLE
FRONT PRESSURE BULKHEAD
ENGINE FRONT MOUNTING
AIR INTAKE ON ENGINE
BRAKE SYSTEM AIR STORAGE CYLINDERS
PLENUM CHAMBER
ENGINE FRONT DRIVE WITH FREE WHEEL DEVICE
'PROTEUS' GAS TURBINE ENGINE - DELIVERING 4,100 SHP AT 11,100 R.P.M. MODIFIED TO DRIVE FROM BOTH ENDS
LIFTING JACKS
CAMERA AND LIGHTS *
HONEYCOMB AUXILIARY BEAMS
BRAKE SYSTEM CHARGING AND JACKING CONTROL PANEL
INTEGRAL LIGHT ALLOY BONDED & RIVETED STRUCTURE
ELECTRICAL SERVICES DISTRIBUTION POINT
AIR BRAKE JACKS
BATTERIES
AIR BRAKE IN EXTENDED POSITION
REAR GEARBOX OIL TANK
PHOTOGRAPHIC INSTRUMENT PANEL
REAR DRIVE SHAFT
ENGINE REAR MOUNTINGS
WISHBONE SUSPENSION ARMS
ENGINE FRONT MOUNTING
ENGINE REAR MOUNTING
AIR BRAKE IN CLOSED POSITION
REAR TOWING EYE
52 DIA x 7·8 TYRES
DISC TYPE STEEL WHEELS WITH DETACHABLE RIMS
REAR PRESSURE BULKHEAD
ELECTRICALLY DRIVEN FUEL & OIL CIRCULATING PUMPS
FUEL TANKS - TOTAL CAPACITY 25 GALLONS
REAR SPIRAL BEVEL GEARBOX RATIO 3·6 TO 1
PNEUMATIC SUSPENSION LEG WITH HYDRAULIC DAMPING
REMOVABLE HONEYCOMB PANEL
CONSTANT VELOCITY COUPLINGS
FOURWAY EXHAUST DUCT WITH SILICA BATT AND ALUMINIUM FOIL INSULATION
INDEPENDENT WISHBONE SUSPENSION ON ALL FOUR WHEELS

The use of honeycomb sandwich in the chassis structure resulted in considerable weight savings, coupled with great strength and stiffness. This was demonstrated when the car turned over during a record attempt at Utah. At the time of the accident, the car was travelling at over 300 mph, and the chassis structure was instrumental in saving Donald Campbell's life.

The manufacture of the honeycomb-sandwich components was carried out by CIBA (ARL), who also manufactured the honeycomb and the film adhesives used. The car was built by Motor Panels Ltd of Coventry.

This technically-advanced vehicle was to become world famous, and in 1964 it set a new world land-speed record of 403.1 mph. The car is now on permanent display at the National Motor Museum in England.

Above One of Bluebird's auxiliary beams after bonding

Top The gearbox cover about to go into the autoclave. Note the vacuum bag which, in this case, is held in place by clamps

Above right One of Bluebird's gearbox covers in the course of construction

Right The two main beams after bonding by CIBA (ARL), now CIBA-GEIGY

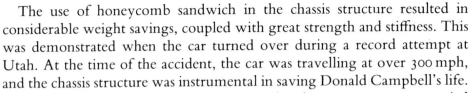

Right This photograph shows the skeletal formation of the chassis, the positions of the main and auxiliary beams being clearly visible

Right The 'egg-box' construction of the chassis can be clearly seen in this photograph of the car, taken during assembly at Motor Panels of Coventry

Left Redux adhesive was used by Girling to bond the rubber and metal components together for these suspension components

2   Benetton Formula

Benetton Formula began life as the renowned Toleman Group Motorsport team, which started racing sucessfully in Formula Two. This involvement led to a full Formula One set-up in 1981. Designer Rory Burns had begun the design of the first Formula One Toleman, the TG181, in 1980. This car was to use the Hart turbocharged engine and was completed and tested early in 1981.

The TG181 was to make widespread use of modern composites. In fact, this new design utilized composites in more components than any other first-time user described in this book. The chassis, or monocoque, was designed around the use of aluminium skins bonded on to aluminium honeycomb, but this sandwich structure did not follow the earlier practice of being formed from pre-made flat panels. Instead, it was made from pre-shaped aluminium skins bonded on to the honeycomb with epoxy film adhesive. Inserts and hard points were incorporated in the chassis lay-up and, again unlike other early designs, took advantage of the extra consolidating pressure offered by an autoclave during the elevated temperature cure. The bulkheads were also aluminium-skinned, aluminium-honeycomb sandwich structures, made separately and bonded in place as another stage, using cold-set, two-part epoxy adhesive.

Structural use was also made of aluminium-skinned honeycomb as the rear-wing mounting pylon, a highly-stressed component. Also, a similar sandwich structure was used for the underwings and side fences, skin material, core type, thickness etc being selected to meet the design requirements of these components, which need great structural stiffness.

The rear-wing end plates were manufactured from carbon fibre bonded on to polyamide-foam core material. This form of construction was also used to make experimental engine mounting plates, and laminated carbon-fibre pre-preg was used to manufacture experimental engine mounting legs. However, the method and materials used in these two experimental areas were not continued in the next car design.

In 1982 the TG182 appeared. This car had a monocoque, or chassis, constructed from aluminium-skinned, aluminium honeycomb by the same method as the previous model. The rear-wing end plates were of the same construction as on the TG181, but one interesting material change was in the underwing and the side fences, where the aluminium-honeycomb core material was changed in favour of Nomex honeycomb, although the skins were still carbon fibre. The body panels of this, and the previous model, were in wet lay-up GRP.

A new model, the TG183(A), was designed and built and appeared at the end of 1982. This new car was to demonstrate a significant advance in the use of composites by Toleman, and that was the utilization of carbon fibre as the monocoque skin material. However, the new chassis still used aluminium honeycomb as a core material, the skins in some areas being of woven carbon pre-preg, with UD pre-preg being used strategically to obtain the required stiffness.

The method used by Toleman consisted of making the chassis in top and bottom halves, each half being laid up in female tooling and cured under vacuum. The two halves were assembled to form the monocoque as another operation, carbon-fibre-skinned honeycomb bulkheads being made as separate items and incorporated at the monocoque assembly stage.

The rear-wing end plates were carbon-skinned foam, similar to previous models, and the underwings were aluminium-skinned Nomex honeycomb, whereas the underwing frames were carbon-fibre-skinned Nomex, as were the side panels. Carbon-fibre-skinned Nomex sandwich structures were utilized in the side fences.

Another important step in the use of modern composites on this model was the use of carbon fibre over Nomex honeycomb for the construction of the nose box. This important structure is the front extension of the monocoque and carries the front wings. It also serves to protect the driver's feet in the event of frontal impact.

The car also had two other very interesting components that utilized carbon fibre. One was the engine inlet plenum, which was tested at 60 psi, and the other was the turbo inlet duct. Bodywork on this model was still made from wet lay-up GRP.

All models were full ground-effect cars, but the TG183(A) was to be the last, since changes in the regulations were to force the return of flat-bottom designs with an enforced ground clearance to prevent the use of ground effect. The outcome was an enforced model change during 1983, the resultant model being the TG183(B).

By this time, composite technology experience gained by Toleman Group Motorsport was being fully utilized, as the TG183(B) shows. This was the first of their cars to use Kevlar.

The monocoque utilized similar materials and manufacturing methods to the previous model, but on this flat-bottomed car, the highly-stressed main underwing was replaced with an undertray. This component still employed a sandwich structure, which consisted of a mixture of carbon and Kevlar in pre-preg form, cured on to Nomex honeycomb under vacuum as a one-shot operation.

The rear-wing end plates on this model changed in configuration and became supports for the wing. To meet their structural requirements, the frequently-used foam core was replaced with Nomex honeycomb, the skins forming the sandwich being carbon-fibre pre-preg, hot cured under vacuum.

Aluminium skins on Nomex formed the front underwings, and carbon-skinned Nomex was used for the front side plates. The same materials were again used for the nose box, and laminated carbon fibre formed the engine inlet plenum and turbo compressor inlet duct.

The TG183(B) was the first model from this company to utilize Kevlar and Nomex for the bodywork, the components being made in female tools and again cured under vacuum. This produced bodywork that was both stiffer and lighter than that of earlier cars.

The new car was to improve on the team's previous best Grand Prix placings of a tenth and fifteenth by recording 12 finishes, including two fourth places and two fifth places, as well as sixth, seventh, eighth and thirteenth placings.

The following season, 1984, was the year of the TG184. This car's monocoque, apart from detail changes, remained very similar in configuration and method of manufacture to the previous model, as did the rear-wing end plates, nose box and bodywork. However, with composite technology continuing to make inroads on race-car design, innovations on this model were the use of Nomex core with carbon-fibre skins for both front and rear wings, carbon fibre to form the tubular front-wing spar, and laminated carbon-fibre pre-preg for the side louvre panels. All these components were hot cured under vacuum.

That year was significant, with two sixth places, a fourth, two thirds and a second.

For the 1985 season, the new TG185 had a completely fresh design and method of manufacture for the monocoque. This was to utilize woven carbon, Kevlar and UD carbon pre-pregs. The woven material was to give the required stiffness. Both aluminium and Nomex honeycomb were

In addition to the Ford Cosworth engine fitted to the Benetton Formula One car, this photograph clearly shows the carbon-fibre roll-over hoop which is moulded as an integral part of the monocoque

In this shot of the Benetton car's engine bay, various composite components can be seen. In the foreground is a carbon-fibre duct, below the turbo is the undertray, and on the left the carbon-composite rear wing

employed, the Nomex in areas with complex shapes, and the aluminium in flat areas.

With the use of split tooling, the monocoque main shell was made in one piece, which was a major change in manufacturing method. The bulkheads were still made separately, however, and bonded in as another stage.

There were two other very significant changes on this new monocoque. One was that, for the first time, the roll hoop was moulded in carbon as an integral part of the structure, offering even greater driver protection. The other was another first, in that the monocoque was body shaped, eliminating the need for frontal body panels.

Technology was taken a stage further with the development of the nose box to meet the new crash-test requirement. To achieve the required performance, the nose-box design utilized aluminium honeycomb and Kevlar pre-preg. A mixture of Kevlar and carbon formed the skins on Nomex honeycomb for the sandwich-construction front wings, which were carried on a tubular spar made from carbon. Kevlar and carbon again formed the skins on Nomex honeycomb for the top, middle, and lower rear wings, and carbon on Nomex was used for the rear-wing end plates.

Other composite components on this model were manufactured in a similar manner to those of the previous car, i.e. Kevlar and Nomex rear body panels, laminated-carbon side louvre panels, and carbon-and-Kevlar-skinned Nomex undertray.

Above The beautiful lines of the 1986 Benetton 198 can be seen in this shot, taken during the Austrian GP

Below The 1986 Benetton from another angle, emphasizing the very clean lines again

All the cars described so far were powered by the turbocharged Hart engine.

It was during the 1985 season, when the team was running the TG185, that Benetton were to purchase the company and become team principals, racing under the now famous name Benetton Formula.

In 1986 the TG186 was to display layout changes to the monocoque to accommodate the BMW engine, which was to be the new powerplant. The materials and method of manufacture followed very similar lines to the previous model, as did those of the remaining composite components.

During the 1986 season, the Benetton team were to show their com-

Above Benetton holding first place during the Austrian GP, illustrating the very competitive level this team reached during the 1986 season

Below The 1987 Benetton Formula One car is almost all composite, from the front wings to the highly-stressed rear wing

petitiveness with several Grand Prix placings, including sixth place twice, fifth twice, and a third. Furthermore, they were to achieve their aim by recording their first Grand Prix win.

This team's case history is classic, in that it shows a progressive approach to composite technology, borne out by the design of the current car, which has utilized available modern composites to the full. Race wise, they have progressed from a humble beginning to the current competitive and exciting team. This technical and competitive achievement is a credit to Rory Bryne, the designer, Phil Henderson on the composite front, and all those who make up this team.

3 Cooper

During the early to mid-1960s, Cooper were the first company to design and build a Formula One chassis that was totally structurally dependent on honeycomb. Designed by Owen Maddock, it consisted of an aluminium outer skin, a GRP inner skin and an aluminium honeycomb core.

The aluminium outer skin was formed as a series of panels by rolling and shaping, using normal panel-beating techniques, and they included flanged edges which served to seal the honeycomb edges. The panels were joined to produce a one-piece outer skin, which had the final aerodynamic

Without doubt, Cooper were the first to use honeycomb for structural purposes in a Formula One racing-car chassis, or monocoque. The material make-up can be clearly seen: a formed aluminium outer skin, aluminium honeycomb and the film adhesive used to bond the two together

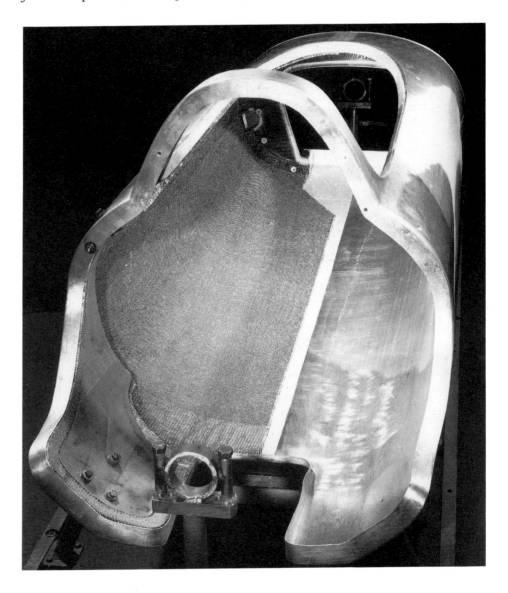

shape of the car. This skin then had aluminium honeycomb bonded to the inside with phenolic adhesive in film form, and was hot cured. The inner skin of GRP was added to form the sandwich as another separate stage.

Unfortunately, this revolutionary chassis design was not to reach the complete car stage and, therefore, there are no tests or performance details. It is interesting to note, however, that this was not only a very early attempt to fully utilize modern composites, but that the chassis exterior shape required no additional bodywork. It was to be almost another 20 years before Formula One chassis were designed to require no further bodywork. In both respects, therefore, the Cooper was many years ahead of its time.

The finished Cooper sandwich-structure monocoque, complete with resinated-glass inner skin

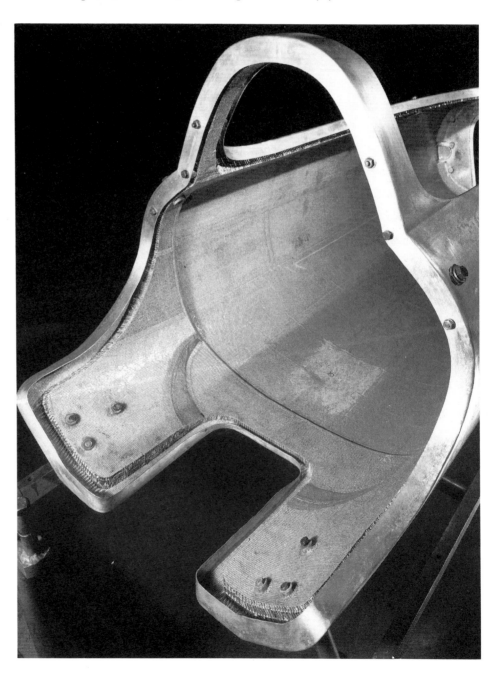

4 Ferrari

Like all competitive Formula One teams, Ferrari utilized wet lay-up glass-fibre components as soon as they became practical and available. In the early years, these components were body panels etc, but full use of modern composites was to follow.

Prior to 1981 the basic chassis design and construction was of a type used only by Ferrari. It consisted of a welded, square-tube space frame, covered with riveted aluminium panels, which, when finished, resembled the single-skin aluminium monocoque that was exclusively used by all other manufacturers immediately before the move to sandwich structures. This panelled space-frame design was modified over the seasons in the search for improved performance. Modifications were usually in the form of additions, i.e. increased cockpit side height, deeper nose section etc.

By 1980 almost all the other Formula One constructors were utilizing sandwich structures in their chassis designs, and some British designers were studying the possible use of carbon fibre as a primary chassis material. Then, in 1981, a staff change at Ferrari was instrumental in the company's rapid utilization of modern composites. This staff change was the arrival of the British designer Dr Harvey Postlethwaite.

Dr Postlethwaite was responsible for the use of carbon fibre on wing end plates and supports on the Hesketh Formula One cars as early as 1974–75, and in 1979 he designed the Wolf Formula One car, which featured a fabricated honeycomb-sandwich monocoque. This used aluminium skins on aluminium honeycomb and, at the time, was considered to be an excellent and advanced monocoque. This composite design experience resulted in Ferrari fielding the 126/C2 car in 1982; the first to utilize modern composites in a significant manner.

The 1982 car had a honeycomb-sandwich monocoque, fabrication being by the cut-and-fold method from pre-made, aluminium-skinned, aluminium-honeycomb sandwich panels. The overall honeycomb sandwich thickness was 25 mm. Performance from the bending and torsional aspects was achieved by a combination of the selected materials in the panel, i.e. skin thickness and type, core type and thickness, and the overall section of the final fabricated shape. All inserts, hard points and mounting points were bonded in after the main chassis was fabricated.

The 126/C2 car was to utilize more composite technology in the under-body, which is another area calling for stiffness and low mass—due to the comparatively large size of the underbody, low mass is extremely important. This first Ferrari to make significant use of modern composites was to win the Constructors' World Championship and give the driver runner-up spot in the Drivers' World Championship.

In 1983 Ferrari extended their composite capability by the addition of an autoclave and a full composite shop. This enabled in-house production of any required components, and the facility was utilized to produce the 126/C3, which had the first fully-composite chassis from Ferrari. The tooling for the composite components was also made by Ferrari in-house.

The new design of chassis was to be shaped to avoid the need for bodywork. To achieve the required external shape, and for other design reasons, the chassis tub was made in a female tool, the chassis floor being made as a separate part and bonded to the tub as another operation. Inserts and mounting points were moulded in during the main chassis lay-up.

The 126/C3 chassis employed honeycomb as a core material to form a sandwich structure, with a combination of carbon and Kevlar skins.

The carbon content of the chassis was in two forms: woven pre-preg as the basis, with UD fibres used strategically. (In this way the design utilized fibre direction to achieve the optimum performance exactly where required.)

The Kevlar content of the chassis laminate was in the form of a complete pre-preg layer, which served as the previously-described fail-safe. In an accident that was severe enough to cause a structural breakdown of the carbon content, the Kevlar would offer some retained structural integrity to prevent complete fragmentation.

This car, the first Ferrari with a carbon-composite chassis, was again to win the Constructors' World Championship.

This 1986 Ferrari is shown next to the large autoclave used by the team to cure composite components

The basic chassis form remained for the following season, but the use of composites was extended to include the engine cover, underbody and nose cone. However, one significant step taken by Ferrari in 1984 was the use of composites in the engine. The parts in question were divisional components in the sump and pump bodies, such as the scavenge pump. They were made from carbon, which has a low coefficient of expansion and low weight, rendering the material suitable for selected engine components.

In 1985 Ferrari were to make advances in tooling development, which is important to composite use. This led to more advanced constructional techniques. The entire car was becoming composite orientated, although the basic chassis construction method was similar to that of the previous year—this car was runner-up in the Championship.

This and the following series of photographs show the moulds and stages in the construction of a Ferrari monocoque. In this particular case, the mould for the bottom half of the monocoque is shown

The mould for the top half of the monocoque

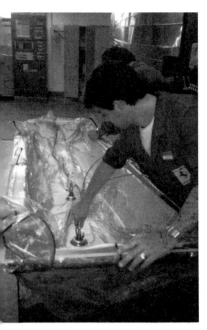

Above The top-half mould with the vacuum bag in place. Note the dark strips of sealing compound used to hold the bag to the mould and to seal the tucks and folds that are necessary when making a shaped bag from a flat sheet. This mould is now ready for the autoclave cure

Top right The monocoque top-half mould with composite lay-up in place

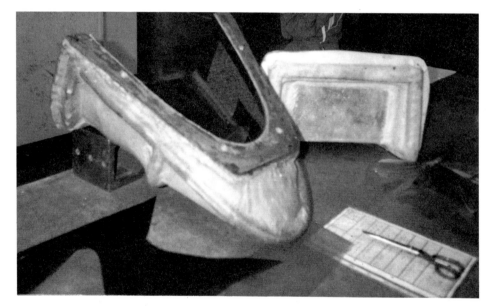

Above right The female mould used to form the Ferrari's composite nose section

Right The monocoque assembled from the top and bottom halves

The finished monocoque awaiting assembly into a complete car. Note the high cockpit sides, which preserve monocoque stiffness

By the following year, a new composites factory was being utilized to the full by Ferrari to produce their new car. Changes from season to season are inevitable for many reasons, but the basic design and manufacturing methods for the Ferrari Formula One car were again similar to those used in the previous season.

This year was to see yet another significant step for Ferrari; the use of composites in the suspension of the Formula One car. This revolutionary move led to the use of carbon fibre in conjunction with some metal to produce suspension arms, or wishbones. The results were very stiff, but lower-mass components in a critical area.

The need for Formula One cars to remain competitive will cause inevitable changes in chassis layout, but in the case of Ferrari there have been no significant chassis changes to report. The main changes in chassis construction relate to methods of use. This is due to Ferrari having put extensive efforts into the development of tooling and constructional methods for modern composites. Apart from the changes mentioned, the basic overall chassis design and material selection have shown little change since the first carbon chassis in 1983.

The race-winning capability of Ferrari's composite Formula One cars needs no explaining, and the immense effort to utilize composites illustrated here will ensure that composites and Ferrari will continue together in the production of their renowned competitive cars.

5 Ford UFO 2 Project

Ford's UFO 2 mileage marathon car, showing the two-piece body/chassis unit made from a combination of composite materials which provided the necessary strength with the minimum of weight

One competition car that did not have the same performance requirements as a formula race car (in fact, it did not race at all as such) was still designed to be totally dependent on modern composites. The car in question was entered by Ford in the Shell mileage marathon, an annual event to establish the vehicle that can complete the greatest distance on a metered quantity of petrol.

To achieve the optimum distance from the fuel, an engine of only 15 cc was used, and with such a small engine the vehicle mass, or weight, was critical. This was kept to a minimum by making the entire chassis and body from combinations of glass, carbon and Kevlar pre-preg, with Nomex honeycomb in some areas as a sandwich structure.

The basic structure was made in two pieces; that is a bottom half and a top half, the bottom forming the chassis on to which the engine and running gear were fitted, and the top being the body. Both parts were suitably shaped to form the required aerodynamic structure when assembled. They were made in female tools to ensure a good outer-surface finish, and the cure was carried out in an autoclave.

The structural bottom half was very cleverly designed to make optimum use of the available composite materials by achieving the required performance from the component with the minimum of weight penalty. Its contoured shape was a sandwich structure, having Nomex honeycomb as a core material, the outer skin being Kevlar pre-preg, and the inner skin a mixture of Kevlar and glass pre-pregs. To achieve the required stiffness, this clever design utilized a second sandwich structure, consisting of carbon-fibre pre-preg skins on Nomex honeycomb, made as a shaped inner floor. The shape of this floor served to accommodate the reclining driver, and was so designed that where it met and was bonded to the outer shell, longitudinal torsion boxes were formed, resulting in a light, stiff chassis.

The upper half of the body also utilized Kevlar pre-preg as the outer skin, a mixture of glass and Kevlar forming the inner skin of the sandwich structure in the areas where Nomex honeycomb was used for strategic stiffening. Due to skilful use of modern composite materials, the entire chassis and body (without engine and running gear) weighed only 20 lb.

The vehicle won the 1984 mileage marathon at Silverstone and set a new world record of 2803 miles per gallon. Although this record has since been broken, the project will remain a technical credit to all those involved.

6 TWR Jaguar

A development programme that turned the Group A Jaguar XJS into a race and, ultimately, championship winner, in the very capable hands of Tom Walkinshaw, almost certainly led to the programme to develop a car to attack the World Endurance Championship, a series that included the famous Le Mans 24-hour race, significant to all Jaguar enthusiasts. In 1985 the designs were realized when construction of the Jaguar XJR-6 Group C car began.

The XJR-6 story begins with a clean sheet, apart from one prerequisite – the Jaguar V12 engine. Tom Walkinshaw and TWR, in conjunction with Jaguar, were to manage the project, and design was placed in the very capable hands of Tony Southgate. The revolutionary design that emerged was, without doubt, the most technically advanced car of its type to be built at the time.

The chassis design was a major step forward in sportscar construction, since it utilized modern composites to the full. It was based on honeycomb-sandwich construction and took full advantage of the properties of carbon and Kevlar fibres as skin materials in the sandwich construction. These materials were utilized to produce the maximum performance from the structure with the minimum of mass.

The composite-dependent Jaguar Group C car in action

This very advanced sportscar chassis consisted of the car's centre section from behind the driver's bulkhead to the nose bulkhead, and included the roof, sill torsion boxes, floor, seat back and fuel cell, all together forming a one-piece, fully-composite component. Woven carbon pre-preg was utilized as the skin material on the torsion boxes, front bulkhead and roof, while a hybrid of carbon on Kevlar (that is a mixture of both fibre types woven together) was used for the floor, the rear driver's bulkhead and the bulkheads behind the front wheels.

There were two reasons for the use of a hybrid material. In the case of the floor and the rear bulkhead, it was to act as the previously-mentioned fail-safe, but the purpose of the Kevlar behind the front wheels was to utilize its wear-resistant qualities to reduce the erosion caused by road grit thrown up by the tyres.

The complexity and size of the chassis prevented it from being made in one piece, so the component parts—bulkheads, side panels etc—were made separately, mostly in female tools. Woven carbon-fibre pre-preg was used to form the skin material over honeycomb for all the sandwich-structure chassis components, and all were produced using vacuum to apply bonding pressure during the elevated-temperature cure. The individual chassis parts were then bonded together with two-part, cold-set adhesive to make the completed chassis.

This unique design also utilized honeycomb sandwich over the entire body area to produce a low-mass, but very stiff structure. Both qualities are very important on a large body like that of the Jaguar, and also apply to the highly-stressed underbody panels.

Apart from some small ducted panels in the sides, the wing and wheel covers, the main body is made in two pieces; the nose (from the windscreen forward) and the tail (from behind the driver's bulkhead rearward). The panels were made in female moulds to achieve the best possible finish.

The body panel lay-up consisted of woven glass pre-preg over most of each panel, with carbon pre-preg used for stiffening and strengthening specific areas, such as around edge flanges and attachment points. The woven glass pre-preg formed both inner and outer skins on a 6 mm thick Nomex honeycomb. This non-metallic honeycomb was utilized to allow production of complex shapes in the panels. An addition to the lay-up was a layer of Kevlar on the inside of the wheel arches, where its high wear-resistant qualities served to prevent erosion of the bodywork by road grit thrown up by the tyres.

All body panels, like the chassis components, were taken through the elevated-temperature cure cycle under pressure from a vacuum bag. Various other components, such as the nose box, wheel covers, ducting etc, were also made from pre-pregs, each of which was selected to suit the relevant component, and all were hot cured under vacuum.

The completed car appeared late in the 1985 season when it first raced at Mosport in Canada. One Jaguar led the race until a wheel bearing failure caused its retirement, and the second car finished third. At the last race of the season, in Malaysia, one of the Jaguars took second place.

Monza was the venue for the first race of 1986, but a drive-flange failure and a fuel-feed problem retired both cars. However, the car was to prove its potential with an impressive win in the Silverstone 1000 km race. Subsequently, the XJR-6 Jaguar held second place in the famous Le Mans 24-hour race, until a burst tyre destroyed the suspension, while the second car retired with a broken CV joint.

The next outing was at the second round of the German championship, where the Jaguars finished second and third.

After the first full season of racing, TWR submitted the Jaguar XJR-6 to the awards judging panel of the Design Council. The panel assembled at Silverstone to take a close look at the car, and two members were lucky enough to experience three laps of the Grand Prix circuit as passengers with Derek Warwick. This first-hand exposure to ground-effect cornering, and a formal presentation of the XJR-6's design points, were enough to win the Design Council's award for Design Excellence. The panel took into consideration the use of carbon fibre as the principal material, which allowed the car to be constructed with an immensely strong, stiff chassis.

The result is a car which, as it travels faster, generates downforce from its overall shape (the upper and lower surfaces working together), and that downforce enables it to corner faster than its competitors, as was amply demonstrated at Silverstone in May 1986, when the Jaguar of Warwick and Cheever trounced the opposition.

From an advanced technical design to a competitive Group C sportscar in such a short time, the XJR-6 is a tribute to all those concerned with Tom Walkinshaw and TWR.

Just how competitive the Jaguar really was can be judged by its performance over the following seasons. It was to win many races, culminating in a championship.

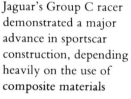

Jaguar's Group C racer demonstrated a major advance in sportscar construction, depending heavily on the use of composite materials

Left The Jaguar chassis in its finished state

Below left The entire load-bearing structure of the car, from the nose bulkhead to just behind the driver's bulkhead is of all-composite construction

Below The front body section of the Jaguar Group C car. This piece, like the rear section, utilized a mixture of carbon and Kevlar as the skin material over a honeycomb core to form a sandwich structure for the entire body. The result was a stiff, light structure. The female mould, in which the front section was made, can be seen in the background

After its very promising debut late in 1985, all eyes were on the XJR-6 for the 1986 season. All this attention was to witness another excellent season for TWR Jaguar Racing, with further progress being made and, in spite of some mid-season problems, the World Sportscar Championship was only decided at the very finish, the title going to Porsche.

Determined development by TWR Jaguar for the 1987 season resulted in a large number of modifications in many areas of the car, but the composite carbon-and-honeycomb chassis was retained in basically the same form. These changes resulted in a new designation: XJR-8. The new car and the new season were to prove sensational.

Unbelievably, the TWR Jaguar XJR-8 won eight of the ten Championship races, giving the team not only the World Sportscar Championship, but first and second places in the World Sportscar Drivers' Championship. Le Mans victory was to elude the team, but with Jaguar picking up two world titles—the first time ever a world title had been won by Jaguar—the season ended with an almost perfect record.

As this was being written, the 1988 season was dawning, and it was evident that TWR Jaguar had been busy, because in addition to their intended continuation of the Group C campaign, they were to give the USA a chance to sample the XJR-9—a TWR Jaguar built to the IMSA formula. The first outing for this new car was at the Sunbank 24-hour race at Daytona, where Porsche's 11-year dominance of the event was shattered, the XJR-9s taking first and third places.

The story of the Jaguar XJRs is yet another clear illustration of the potential of modern composites in the construction of competition vehicles, and it shows just what can be achieved with their use.

7 Lola Cars

Right The all-composite
Lola 610 in its Le Mans
form

For many years, Lola Cars have been world-famous as commercial manufacturers of sports and single-seater racing cars. They have produced race-
winning cars in a wide range of formulae, including Formula One, CART
or Indianapolis, Group C, IMSA, and various sportscar classes. Like all
other racing-car manufacturers, Lola have utilized wet lay-up GRP for
bodywork since its availability, and to retain the renowned Lola competitiveness, full use has been made of modern composites as a follow-on
to wet lay-up resin systems.

Lola's first move towards the use of modern composites came in 1982
on the T850 Formula Two car, where carbon fibre was utilized as a skin
material on aluminium-honeycomb core to form the rear wing and pylon.
Two further significant steps in the use of composites were taken by Lola
that year. The first was the use of honeycomb sandwich panels as the inner
monocoque, or chassis, panels on the T600 IMSA GTP endurance sportscar. These monocoque panels were fabricated from pre-made flat panels
consisting of aluminium skins bonded on to aluminium honeycomb, using
epoxy film adhesive, and hot cured in a press.

The T600 car also utilized modern composites in the venturi underbodies,
which were constructed from laminated glass pre-preg, oven cured under
vacuum on wet lay-up resin-and-glass tooling.

Later in 1982 Lola produced the T610 Group C car. This was a major
step by Lola, as the car was almost certainly the first of such large size to
have not only a composite chassis, but the entire body made from a
sandwich structure. The monocoque was made completely from honeycomb sandwich, the inner and outer panels having aluminium skins, and
the floor panel carbon-fibre pre-preg skins. Aluminium-honeycomb core
was used in all the monocoque panels, which were press cured prior to
assembly into the monocoque form.

The body of the T610 was made from woven glass pre-preg over non-
metallic Nomex honeycomb, the core material being chosen for its better
drapability in the areas of complex shape. Metallic honeycomb was used in
the flatter areas. The large body panels, including the entire nose section
and tail sections, were made in female tools by the one-shot method; that
is both inner and outer skins, together with the honeycomb core, were laid
up and cured in a single operation.

The venturi underbodies were also of sandwich structure, consisting of
glass pre-preg over aluminium honeycomb and made in a single operation
using the same method as for the body panels. Other major components,
such as nose splitter and wings, were made in composite, carbon-fibre pre-
preg being utilized on these highly-stressed components.

Right This view of the Lola
610 clearly shows the
venturi-shaped underside,
which was formed from
glass-fibre pre-preg and
honeycomb. The vertical
deflector panel, in all-
aluminium sandwich, can
also be seen

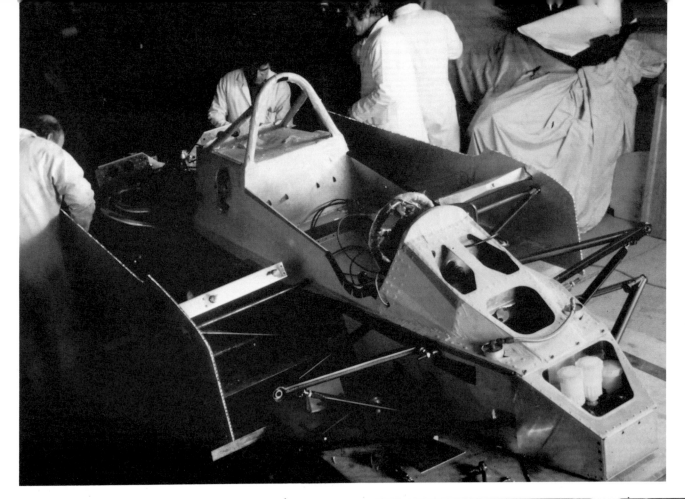

Left An early example of a Lola CART-series car. The chassis is of single-skin aluminium, but the side-pod walls have honeycomb cores and demonstrate the beginning of the company's use of composites

Below left Here is a much later Lola CART racer. The all-aluminium-sandwich, deformable monocoque bottom half is joined to a moulded pre-preg-and-honeycomb top half. The deformable bottom half is to meet the requirements of the American regulations and is not used in Formula One monocoques

Below The Lola T800 CART-series car in its Championship-winning form

Lola's first major use of modern composites in a single seater occurred in 1983. This car was the T700 CART, or Indianapolis, type. The entire monocoque and side pods were fabricated from pre-made flat panels, consisting of aluminium skins on aluminium honeycomb, but wet lay-up, cold-cure GRP was still used for the bodywork.

The company took another major step in 1984 with the T800. For the first time they utilized moulded carbon and Kevlar to form the top half of the monocoque. This moulding consisted of carbon on Kevlar pre-pregs, laid into female tooling to form an inner and outer skin on aluminium honeycomb, and hot cured under vacuum.

It will be noted that only the top half of the monocoque was in the carbon-Kevlar configuration. This was due to the American CART regulations demanding that the lower half of the monocoque had to be a deformable structure. To achieve this, the bottom half was made from flat, pre-made, aluminium-skinned, aluminium-honeycomb panels, in a similar fashion to the method used for the T700 monocoque.

In 1985 Lola produced the T900 CART car, which had a monocoque that, apart from dimensional and shape changes, was similar to the T800, particularly in the method of manufacture. The major change was the use of glass pre-preg, but it was cured under vacuum in female moulds. Another advance in the use of composites on this car was the selection of carbon-fibre pre-preg on non-metallic Nomex honeycomb to produce sandwich-construction underbodies. Again, these were made in one shot and hot cured under vacuum.

That year also saw the production of the T810 IMSA GTP. This had a monocoque that was fabricated from flat, pre-made, aluminium-skinned, aluminium-honeycomb panels, with the exception of the monocoque floor, which utilized carbon fibre for the sandwich skins.

Bodywork for the T810 was executed mainly in glass pre-preg on both aluminium and Nomex non-metallic honeycomb, the latter being utilized in areas of complex shape. Some carbon-fibre pre-preg was used strategically to give local strength or stiffness. Again, underbodies were sandwich structures, using glass pre-preg and carbon fibre strategically. All these components were made in one shot and hot cured under vacuum.

Yet another very progressive step in the use of modern composites was taken in 1986 with the production of the T86/50 Formula 3000 car. Not being bound by regulations demanding a deformable structure, the entire monocoque shell was produced with carbon fibre as the skin material on aluminium honeycomb. As usual, the method was one shot, hot cured under vacuum. The bodywork for this car was laminated from glass pre-preg and hot cured under vacuum in female moulds.

Since they began to utilize modern composites, Lola have produced many cars of different types to suit the various formulae, and those cars are far too numerous to detail every one, but this case history serves to illustrate the major advances as they were made.

Little needs saying about the success enjoyed by cars produced by Lola, but mention must be made of some notable victories. These include the 1982 IMSA GTP, won by the Lola T600. Although the following model, the T610, failed to win the Le Mans 24-hour race, it did have the distinction of being timed as the fastest car on the long straight, at 228 mph. The T800 model won the 1984 CART/Indy series, and the T86/50 won the first round of the 1986 3000 series at Silverstone.

Success in design and production leads to success on the track. For many years, Lola have proved this point, and with the very comprehensive composite facilities that are now a major part of the company, modern composites are likely to be fully utilized in their future car designs.

An unpainted example of a Lola endurance sports car for the American IMSA series. The complex-shaped bodywork is made entirely of pre-preg and honeycomb

8   Team Lotus

Team Lotus, like most other progressive racing teams, passed through the early use of wet lay-up glass-fibre body panels etc, and entered the era of pre-impregnated fibres via various semi-structural and non-structural components. This progression and evaluation of modern composites led to a major step for both Lotus and composite development in 1980. This was the appearance of what is claimed to be the first carbon-fibre composite race-car chassis. At that time, the almost universal method of race-car chassis construction was the single-skin aluminium monocoque, which had superseded the space-frame chassis form.

The last Lotus single-skin monocoque was the successful Lotus 79 Formula One car. This had a chassis that weighed approximately 95 lb and had a torsional stiffness of approximately 3000 lb ft/degree. Chassis development led to higher cockpit sides to improve torsional stiffness and improve driver protection. These improvements, coupled with the use of aluminium-skinned, aluminium honeycomb, produced a chassis that weighed approximately 85 lb with an increase in torsional stiffness to 5000 lb ft/degree. The use of honeycomb and film adhesives can be considered a major contributor to this marked improvement in chassis performance and saving in weight. These observations, together with a long and detailed study, led to the carbon-fibre composite chassis of 1980.

The method of construction was unique. It began with a carbon-and-Kevlar hybrid fabric being wet impregnated on to honeycomb to form a flat sandwich panel. The impregnated lay-up was allowed to reach a 'green', or part-cured, stage, and was then formed around a chassis tool, or mandrel. Next it was post cured to achieve the maximum possible performance from the resin system.

The hybrid material consisted of a woven fabric that was mainly carbon, but had Kevlar fibres at intervals in both directions. The reason for selecting a fabric of this type was to utilize the carbon content to provide strength and stiffness, and the Kevlar to act as a fail-safe. The flexibility of the Kevlar would hold the structure together if an impact was sufficient to cause failure of the carbon.

It is interesting to note that the use of hybrid fabrics (carbon and Kevlar in the same weave) has given way to the use of individual layers of each material. This allows the Kevlar to serve its purpose better in the case of a serious accident.

Lotus took a big step forward in their unique method of chassis construction by the use of pre-impregnated fibres in place of the wet lay-up method of sandwich skin construction. This change to pre-pregs was important from the point of view that it produced skins of constant thickness, and constant designed weight. Achieving designed weight is possible because the most widely used pre-pregs contain few or no volatiles and, therefore, neither gain nor lose weight during the cure. Furthermore, due to the resin systems being fully cross-linked during the elevated-temperature cure cycle, skin laminates are produced consistent to specified performance.

The method of construction, therefore, consisted of the selected pre-preg types and numbers of layers being layed up on each side of the selected honeycomb type, and then placed under vacuum on a flat bed and taken through the recommended cure cycle in an oven.

This chassis type, like its predecessor, was formed around a male tool, or mandrel, but unlike the previous method, the sandwich panel was fully cured and had to be formed using the cut-and-fold technique. Then the chassis was bonded in the same way as the previous type, utilizing adhesive and capping strips. The latter were of a material similar to the chassis skin, formed to cover the panel cuts, and used to restore skin continuity. In this way, optimum performance can be achieved from this type of construction.

Over a four- to five-year period, Team Lotus tested hundreds of samples in an effort to obtain the optimum performance from the materials to achieve high levels of stiffness, strength and, very important, driver protection. This vast amount of test work was necessary to enable the designer to utilize materials that behave in a different way to conventional, or previously-used chassis construction. Pliable aluminium has been replaced with blends of carbon (stiff, but brittle), Kevlar (strong and tough), and honeycomb (skin stabilizer and crush absorber).

Past experience and extensive test work led to the new chassis weighing in at approximately 70 lb with a torsional stiffness of 10,000 ft lb/degree. These figures show the giant strides being made in chassis design.

Team Lotus have taken this technology a stage further by producing later chassis directly in pre-preg. The chassis is still made around a male tool, or mandrel, but the pre-impregnated fibres are applied directly to the tool and not pre-made as a flat panel. This type of structure utilizes pre-pregs and honeycomb in a similar fashion to previous chassis designs, but eliminates the skin joins and, therefore, affords maximum performance from the materials and the design.

Throughout the development of the Lotus carbon chassis, some parts have remained metallic, the main ones being the suspension and engine mounting points, which are machined from aluminium. These serve to spread the loads out on to the chassis and to balance the loads across the car. This system is claimed by Lotus to give the structure a degree of ductility to failure at the chassis hard points, offering considerable protection to the composite structure in the event of an accident.

The machined aluminium components can be in the form of transverse bulkheads, and are attached to the carbon chassis by means of double-sided inserts, or bobbins. Double-sided means that the insert, or bobbin, is put on to the chassis wall from both sides, meeting in the middle of the honeycomb core and resulting in a solid-lined bolt hole that prevents the sandwich structure being crushed under any subsequent clamping pressure. The insert is attached to both skins of the sandwich by means of a thin head that is larger than the part passing through the panel. These heads are bonded to the outer skin on each side of the sandwich with epoxy adhesive. The bonded area of the attachment, coupled with the design of the insert, serves to distribute loads through the panel from both sides—a structurally important point to the designer.

Lotus' method of forming the chassis structure around a male tool produces finished components with accurate inside dimensions, which gives great advantage when fitting machined and removable bulkheads.

The team have utilized their developed skill and composite knowledge in all areas of their race cars; these include bodywork, side pods and underbody components. Their skill was used to the full during the period of the ground-effect Formula One cars, when the underside became very highly-stressed, but the honeycomb sandwich passed this test with flying colours.

The knowledge gained by Lotus in their Formula One development, and particularly chassis design, plus the inevitable test work that led to these designs, has paved the way for their CART programme. This means race cars for American Indianapolis-type racing.

Regulations for the CART series make it mandatory that the lower part of the chassis is a deformable structure. They prevent the total use of carbon

The Lotus 81 shows the very angular body contours of that year's design. Note that aluminium was still being used as a chassis material and can be seen behind the driver

as a chassis material and, therefore, the designer must use aluminium skins on aluminium honeycomb. These still produce a structure of immense stiffness, but the ductile nature of this all-aluminium sandwich provides the necessary deformable structure.

Lotus, and other European race-car constructors, have shown through development the immense performance and safety capabilities of all-fibre chassis design. One day, this may have an effect on the regulations governing cars for the American CART series, where speeds are high and potential impact loads are much greater if an accident occurs.

As a tribute to Team Lotus' design and composite technique, it is interesting to note that since 1980 and the introduction of the carbon chassis, all 23 cars made in this way still survive, not one having been lost in an accident. Whatever race-car regulations demand, the level of development illustrated here by Lotus will ensure that modern composites will be utilized to meet the requirement.

The Lotus 91 shows flowing lines. This composite-based car was of the full ground-effect type

9 McLaren

Like most forward-thinking race-car manufacturers, Team McLaren utilized glass fibre and wet lay-up resin systems for body panels etc in the early years of composites. However, one very revolutionary design for the time appeared in 1965, when Robin Herd designed and built the first McLaren Formula One car to utilize a chassis made from a sandwich structure. This vehicle, known as the Malite car, had a fabricated monocoque assembled from pre-made flat panels.

The panels were made from aluminium skins bonded on to end-grain balsa wood, which formed the core material. The core consisted of selected balsa planks glued together to form a large block, with the wood grain running in one direction. Panels of the required thickness were then cut from this block, across the grain, producing a panel with the wood grain running at right angles to its face. As a core material, end-grain balsa produces a sandwich panel of reasonable stiffness, comparatively light weight and with an exceptional compressive strength-to-weight ratio.

The Malite car did compete for the entire season, but then reverted to a single-skin, aluminium monocoque.

Gordon Coppuck, who was to take over McLaren design, produced an interim stage on the aluminium chassis. This was the injection of rigid-setting polystyrene foam between the skins, tying them together. This car also had fibreglass and aluminium in the side pods. The foam-sandwich construction was raced successfully as the M23, in which James Hunt won the World Championship.

Convinced of the value of sandwich structures, Gordon Coppuck then utilized honeycomb for its higher structural performance. As a result, the M26 was the first McLaren to use honeycomb as a core material. Its chassis was fabricated from a sandwich consisting of aluminium skins bonded on to aluminium honeycomb, using hot-cured film adhesive from the epoxy range.

The M26 was not very successful for McLaren, but the lack of success was not attributed to the overall design, rather to many other reasons that can render a Formula One car uncompetitive.

It is evident that Gordon Coppuck realized the potential of honeycomb sandwich, as the next car, the M28, was the first full honeycomb chassis from this stable. This design progressed to a new method of construction. Although still aluminium-skinned, aluminium honeycomb, the structure consisted of preformed skins placed on to a male tool, together with the selected type of honeycomb, and epoxy film adhesive between the skins and core. The entire chassis was then hot cured in one shot, a vacuum bag supplying the necessary pressure for bonding.

The McLaren M26 was an early example of the team's use of honeycomb sandwich. In this case, the monocoque was made with aluminium skins over aluminium honeycomb

Another very advanced step in the M28's chassis construction was that all the inserts, or hard points, including the engine mounts, were bonded in at the same time as the main structure was formed, each insert being held accurately in place by pegs in the male tool.

The next car, the M29, still retained an all-aluminium sandwich construction, but reverted to being fabricated from pre-made panels. This was not for structural reasons, but because the previous method proved to be extremely time consuming and, due to the complicated tooling required, made it difficult to effect quick or simple changes to the chassis.

There were to be enforced technical advances for the following model, the M30, as this was the first full ground-effect car. This meant that the car was much closer to the ground and had a suitably designed, aerodynamic underside that, at speed, produced a partial vacuum under the car. This helped to hold the car firmly down; in fact, it was sucked on to the road, resulting in much faster cornering speeds.

To utilize ground effect, the car had to have little or no travel on the suspension, which led to side skirts being fitted to the body sides that were in contact with the road to ensure maximum effect from the downforce.

The chassis of this car continued to be fabricated from pre-made, aluminium-skinned, aluminium-honeycomb panels, but advances were made in the design of the aerodynamic underside. This panel not only had to be of the optimum shape to produce the downforce but, due to the immense loads produced at high speed, had to be extremely stiff to resist being sucked down and out of shape. Also, due to its large size, it needed to be of light weight.

McLaren again utilized honeycomb for the panel but, due to its aerodynamic shape, took a major step forward by laying glass pre-preg directly

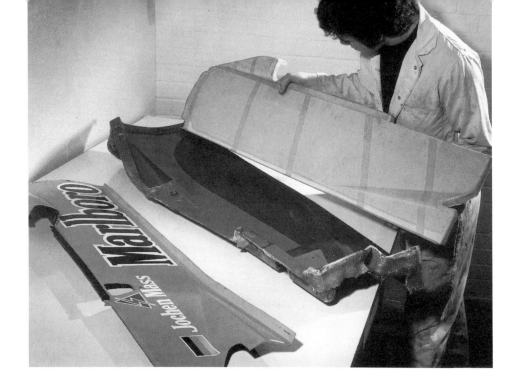

Here is a typical piece of race-car bodywork, both in the finished state and direct from the mould, which is also shown. The component consists of glass-fibre pre-preg over honeycomb, and the dark lines are strips of carbon fibre which have been added to provide stiffness

on to the honeycomb and curing it under a vacuum bag in one operation. The tooling on which this undertray was made was a cast-resin mould, utilizing tooling resin capable of withstanding the temperatures required to cure the pre-preg used in the component. Past experience of making smaller, strength-dependent components, such as a wing, end plates, radiator ducting etc, served to give McLaren the skill and confidence to take this major step.

The undertrays were to prove very successful, both from the aerodynamic and strength aspects. The same method of undertray construction was employed by most of the Formula One teams, although different combinations of pre-preg and honeycomb were utilized. Again, this indicates the versatility of modern composites.

In 1980 the company changed in both name and design staff. The new name was McLaren International Ltd, and the new technical director was J.E. Barnard. In the previous year, Project Four Ltd had decided to enter Formula One, and a design team, headed by John Barnard, had been set up to design and build a car. This project was to go to McLaren with the merger of the two companies.

With design targets set to achieve at least a 66 per cent increase in nominal torsional stiffness, coupled with a reduction in mass, and with the current method of chassis construction well exploited, the design team set out to evaluate the use of carbon composite.

It is interesting to note that although most of the modern composite technology at that time was considered to be available in Europe, and the UK in particular, manufacturing support for the project was not forthcoming. Fortunately, Hercules, in the USA, took the opportunity to support the project and carried out the manufacture of the new design. The resultant carbon-composite chassis was the now famous MP4.

The monolithic design aimed to utilize carbon fibre to the maximum by maintaining fibre continuity wherever possible throughout the structure, and keeping the post moulding joints to a minimum ensured that design

Another Marlboro McLaren composite-dependent car was the 1985 MP4/2B Tag Turbo, which was driven by three-times World Champion Niki Lauda. The monocoque for this model was moulded from carbon fibre over a honeycomb core

Above right Taken during the 1986 Italian Grand Prix, this photograph shows the composite-dependent Marlboro McLaren MP4/2C Tag Turbo

Right The wide use of composites in the MP4/2C can be clearly seen in this photograph. The carbon-fibre monocoque, side-pod structure and the undertray, beneath the gearbox, are visible

stiffness was maintained. The honeycomb throughout the chassis was of constant thickness. This served to eliminate discontinuity in the lay-up and, again, contributed to maintained stiffness. Throughout the chassis all load-bearing attachment points were moulded in, thus avoiding the use of potted inserts, i.e. inserts put in after the chassis had been made.

The MP4 chassis consisted of five major structural components: left- and right-hand cockpit inner walls, a seat bulkhead, steering bulkhead, and the main tub, or chassis, into which the other components were bonded, using cold-setting, two-component epoxy adhesive. Tack bolts at approximately 70 mm pitch were used as crack stoppers, designed to prevent bond failures propagating in the event of a crash.

The chassis components of the MP4 were bonded on male tooling, claimed by the designer to give the opportunity for total consolidation of the laminated lay-up. The cure was carried out in an autoclave to ensure that sufficient pressure was applied to consolidate a complex composite shape.

Another important point is that the temperature used for the cure was 175 degrees Celsius. This was due to the performance requirement necessitating the use of pre-preg materials which had a cure temperature in this range. The use of this higher than normal temperature necessitated special, high-temperature-resistant tooling, and cast aluminium, machined to size and shape, was chosen.

In addition to aluminium-honeycomb core materials, the MP4 chassis utilized woven and UD carbon-fibre pre-pregs. The woven material served as a base material, and the UD fibres were employed strategically; that is performance was enhanced in the required areas of the chassis by controlling the fibre direction.

From an engineering point of view, John Barnard's MP4 chassis was very advanced, especially as it was totally dependent on modern composites. It proved so successful that the basic design remained unchanged for the first six seasons of use, which is exceptional in Formula One racing.

The McLaren MP4/2C in action

Marlboro McLaren's winning team in the 1984 Formula One World Championship. Composites played a major part in that success

McLaren's detailed analysis of the MP4 chassis over the years showed one extremely important fact, and that is structural stability. The last aluminium monocoque that preceded the MP4 could be expected to show a 30 per cent drop in stiffness over a season's racing. The carbon MP4 showed a maximum of 5 per cent loss of torsional stiffness over three seasons, and in some cases this level was maintained after chassis repairs had been carried out. This must prove to be another major advantage of the monolithic carbon-fibre design.

The composite expertise gained during the design and building of the MP4 chassis has been utilized to full advantage by McLaren to produce other highly-stressed components, such as undertrays and wings. Prior to the MP4, skirts and under-wing panels had been manufactured in wet-lay-up materials, sometimes as a sandwich using foam as a core material. Due to increasing aerodynamic loading and the requirement to control the accuracy of underside profiles, the use of pre-pregs and honeycomb was essential to allow the design to meet those requirements, especially during the 1981–82 period with the ground-effect cars. With the return to the flat-bottomed cars, underbody forces were reduced for a given area, but the flat-bottom underbody was a larger one-piece panel, so the stiffness requirement remained, and the sandwich-structure knowledge was utilized to good effect.

The other highly-stressed components where carbon composites have been utilized are wings, mainly the rear wing and flap. A conservative load figure of 1250 lb can be expected on these items and, therefore, high strength and stiffness are required, while keeping the mass low. Again, modern composites enable the designer to achieve his aim.

It is not necessary to illustrate McLaren's race-winning capability, but their utilization of modern composites must be applauded, not only in design but also in manufacture. From 1985 the entire composite production, including the chassis, took place in-house.

Above This photograph of Alain Prost's Renault clearly shows the carbon composite chassis, or monocoque. The fabricated metallic nose box can also be seen supporting the front wings

Overleaf, left This 1987 Benetton Formula One car shows that composites not only produce high-performance structures, but also aerodynamic shapes without the need for additional bodywork

Overleaf, right Dr Harvey Postlethwaite (right) with Lorenzo Panini, sitting in front of Ferrari's autoclave, which was built by the latter. This greatly extended the team's use of composites in their cars

Two views of the Ford UFO 2
project vehicle. The lower
photograph shows the
moulded carbon–fibre inner
panel, which forms the
torsion–box stiffening area

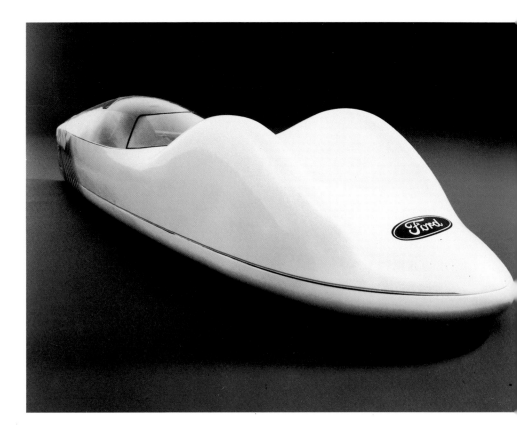

The very advanced Jaguar
sportscar. The entire chassis
assembly, including the roof,
is structural and is totally
dependent on carbon-fibre
skins over a honeycomb core

Above Armstrong's CF250 made its debut in 1983 with a unique all-composite chassis and rear fork made from carbon-fibre-skinned honeycomb material

Right The functional Armstrong chassis showing the weave of the carbon fibre and the bonded-in hard points

Left This Lotus 97 CART-series car clearly shows the extent of the team's use of modern composites. The carbon-and-Kevlar monocoque layout is evident, as are the honeycomb-sandwich side pods. The front and rear wings are also of composite materials

Right Nigel Leaper's revolutionary composite-based motorcycle chassis which appeared in 1984 on the Heron Suzuki Project 500. It was made from aluminium-skinned, aluminium honeycomb

Below The bike that never was. Nigel Leaper's design for the 1987 V4-engined Heron Suzuki, which was dropped in favour of a conventional aluminium chassis when Suzuki themselves resumed the GP road-racing effort

10 Motor Racing Developments (Brabham)

Brabham first used modern composites in 1979 on the BT48 Formula One car, when they employed some small, hot-cured, pre-preg-laminate panels as skins on an all-riveted, mainly aluminium monocoque. Laminated pre-pregs were also utilized on the ground-contact skirts which were in use at that time.

In 1981 the type progressed to the BT49C. This model had the same monocoque as the BT48, but the team made further use of modern composites in the form of a carbon-fibre-skinned, aluminium-honeycomb underwing, hot cured in one shot under vacuum on GRP tooling. The skirts, now of rigid form, were still in laminated pre-preg. This car was to produce a world champion.

The next year saw the arrival of the BT50 model, in which the BMW engine replaced the Ford Cosworth. Apart from minor dimensional changes, this car was structurally the same as the BT49C.

In 1983 a comprehensive composite facility was completed, and a new car, the BT52, appeared. This was to use considerably more composites in its construction than previous models. The monocoque consisted of a

The 1983 Brabham BT52

fabricated bottom half, being made from sheet aluminium with some honeycomb forming a sandwich structure in the fuel-cell area. The top half of the monocoque was of carbon pre-preg in a laminated-only form. GRP female tooling was used to mould this component. The elevated-temperature cure was carried out in an autoclave, allowing a much higher bonding pressure to be used than was possible by vacuum. Higher pressure serves to consolidate the laminated skin of the sandwich structure.

Consolidation of the skin serves two purposes; it optimizes the structural performance of the selected composite material and, generally, the higher bonding pressure produces a better aesthetic finish—but this is not a golden rule. The high cost of running autoclaves, coupled with much longer cycle times, due to there being a large mass to heat up and cool down, are reasons why the components selected for autoclave cures are, in many cases, structurally-dependent components. Again, however, this is not a golden rule.

The BT52's monocoque inner panel was a laminate of carbon and Kevlar, the pre-preg also being cured in female tooling. The underwing, being highly-stressed, was a sandwich-structure component, utilizing carbon-fibre pre-preg skins on Nomex honeycomb. Other composite components on this car included the front wings and flaps. The method of construction for these comprised carbon-fibre pre-preg skins on profiled foam

The Brabham BT55 (left) shows a much lower configuration and driver position than the previous BT54 model

cores, which were shaped by the hot-wire method. The skins were made as a thin laminate and bonded on to the foam core as a second operation. The rear winglets were made by the same method.

The rear wing, being a very highly-stressed component, again utilized Nomex honeycomb as a core material, with carbon-fibre skins to give the required strength. Body panels, such as the engine cover, were laminated carbon, hot cured in female tools, the laminate thickness being controlled to give sufficient stiffness and strength with a minimum mass.

This very successful car was to enable Nelson Piquet to win the Drivers' World Championship.

The following year, 1984, was the season of the BT53. Apart from aerodynamic and geometric changes, and the use of honeycomb as a core material for the front wing, the method of construction for this car was similar to that for the BT52. However, carbon fibre was used for the tooling.

The BT54 took over in 1985. Again, there were aerodynamic and geometric changes, but the overall method of construction remained the same as for the previous car. Of interest was the fact that the design of the front wings moved away from the complex delta shape seen on previous models to a more conventional arrangement.

In 1986 the BT55 was built to a completely fresh design, using a new method of construction. This car had the much-publicized very low profile; that is the overall height of the car was much lower than all previous models from this stable, or any other, putting the driver in a much more pronounced, reclined driving position. Matching the revolutionary appearance of the car, the method of monocoque construction was equally unusual.

The BT55's monocoque was constructed as a one-piece, seamless, carbon-fibre-and-Kevlar skin on non-metallic Nomex honeycomb. Another significant point was that in all previous carbon-fibre monocoque constructions, the components were manufactured in female tooling, and the same method was used to achieve the seamless configuration of the monocoque.

An interesting point to note is that Motor Racing Developments (Brabham) used alloy bulkheads on all their carbon-fibre monocoques, including that of the BT55. These were bonded into place after the composite shell had been completed. By comparison, in many cases, their competitors used composite bulkheads, either bonded in after completion of the basic shell, or sometimes as integral bulkheads.

Further use of carbon pre-pregs was made on the BT55 for the engine air intakes and the air cooling ducts. The remaining components—the front and rear wings, wing end plates, underwing etc—were manufactured in similar materials and by similar methods to the previous model, although there were dimensional changes.

Motor Racing Developments (Brabham) have always been at the forefront of competition, both on the track and in the technology race. During the period since the utilization of modern composites, two World Championships and many pole positions pay tribute to the designs of Gordon Murray and the overall company leadership of Bernie Ecclestone.

This view of the Brabham BT55 clearly shows the layout of the carbon-fibre monocoque and undertray

11 Reynard Racing

As part of their competition-car output, Reynard Racing produce single-seater cars for the highly-competitive Formula Three class, this being the breeding ground for many of the current world's best Formula One drivers. Formula Three racing does not carry the huge sponsorship associated with Formula One and CART series and, therefore, from the production point of view, is a commercial proposition. To some extent, this commercial aspect could control the level of composite technology utilized.

Among the leading manufacturers in this competitive area, Reynard Racing produce a Formula Three monocoque that is very advanced technically and totally dependent on the use of modern composites. It consists

The Formula Three Reynard in action and in its championship-winning form

Right A Reynard Formula
Three carbon-fibre and
honeycomb monocoque
nearing completion

Below The Reynard works,
showing Formula Three
monocoques in production
and proving that the high-
technology use of pre-pregs
and honeycomb is not
restricted to one-off or
limited-production
components. The success of
the company's cars proves
their quality

of carbon and Kevlar skins on honeycomb for the main shell, with carbon-fibre-skinned honeycomb bulkheads and an aluminium monocoque floor added as separate stages. The main shell utilizes woven carbon and Kevlar pre-pregs with UD carbon pre-preg in specific areas to achieve the required stiffness.

For technical reasons, the monocoque sandwich structure's outer skin is formed in female tooling as a first stage, and the elevated-temperature cure is carried out under vacuum. The honeycomb core and inner, or sandwich, skin are also cured under vacuum as a second stage. As in all cases where the outer skin is cured separately, a film adhesive is necessary between this pre-cured skin and the remainder of the lay-up (the honeycomb and the inner skin).

This advanced car also utilizes carbon-fibre-skinned honeycomb as a means of constructing both front and rear wings. The rear under-diffuser duct is of a pre-preg-and-honeycomb construction, as is the front floor area, which employs glass-pre-preg-skinned honeycomb to meet the performance requirements. The remaining composite components on the car are the wing end plates, which are sandwich structures that use woven-glass pre-preg skins with strategically-placed UD pre-preg to achieve the required performance.

The advanced technology utilized in the Reynard has proved its worth since its adoption in 1984. The car showed its competitiveness from the beginning, and its 1985 season's successes included the British Championship, European Championship, Swedish Championship, and the Formula Three World Cup. This level of success within two years must have been due, in part, to the versatility of modern composites, but most of all, it is a great tribute to Reynard Racing and all those connected with the production of this very successful car.

12 Williams GP Engineering

Williams' introduction to modern composites occurred as early as the 1978–79 Formula One season on the FW06 model, which utilized glass-and-epoxy pre-preg skins, hot cured on to a foam core to produce rear-wing end plates. These early components were bought in.

In 1980 the FW07B had similar rear-wing end plates to the previous model, but this car was to extend the team's use of composites by having its side panels manufactured from glass pre-preg on aluminium honeycomb. These sandwich-structure components had an excellent stiffness-to-weight ratio.

The FW07C, of 1981, was to use aluminium honeycomb in some areas of the alloy monocoque, the tank top and part of the side panels to enhance stiffness. Another new area of composite use was the rear wing, where the fabricated-aluminium method of construction gave way to carbon-fibre pre-preg skins on a foam core, again producing a strong, light component. Strength was a very important factor on this highly-stressed component. The method of manufacture for this rear wing was to profile foam by the hot-wire technique, then to bond on the pre-made carbon-laminated skin as a second operation.

In 1982 the FW08 appeared. This model was the first to have a complete monocoque fabricated from aluminium-skinned, aluminium-honeycomb panels. The remaining components were constructed in a similar manner to those of the previous season's model. The composite additions on this car were the front wings and underwing.

The front wings were carbon-fibre pre-preg on a profiled foam core, which was shaped by the widely-used hot-wire method. The underwing was also a sandwich structure, consisting of carbon pre-preg skins on Nomex honeycomb, hot cured on resin tooling in one shot. The cure took place under vacuum.

The FW08C, which appeared in 1983, was another model of similar overall construction. Composites, however, were to make further inroads on the materials used for component construction. The composite rear wing had flaps made by the same method as that used for the front wings; that is carbon-fibre pre-preg skins on profiled foam, cured by the two-shot method.

Another big step forward on the FW08C was the addition of carbon pre-preg to the fabricated alloy side pods to serve as wheel fairings. These were made in female resin tools, the elevated-temperature cure being carried out under vacuum by the one-shot method—no honeycomb was used.

Williams built two models for 1984, the FW09 and the FW09B. Geometric and dimensional changes necessitated the model change, and this is

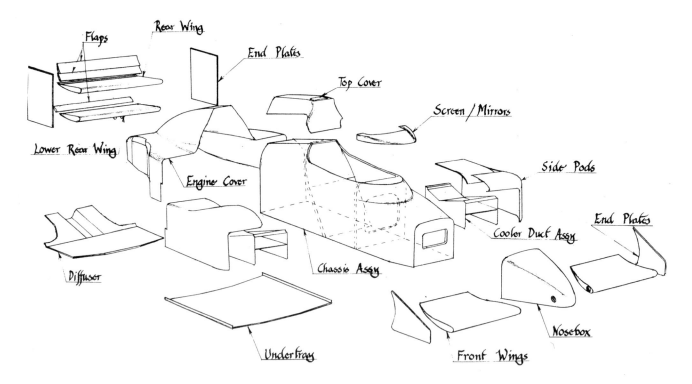

The composite components used in a Williams FW10 Formula One car

an example of how modern composites enable the designer to effect the required changes to achieve the performance necessary from any component, or the complete car.

Both models were manufactured by similar methods and from similar materials, but after another season both were to have yet more components manufactured from modern composites. These new areas of composite use were the fuel-cell top panel and the box forming the nose of the car, which is a removable extension of the monocoque. Also of composite construction were the side pods.

The fuel-cell top was a sandwich structure of carbon skins on Nomex honeycomb, hot cured under vacuum in one shot. The nose box on the FW09 was a sandwich of carbon and Nomex, while that on the FW09B utilized carbon as a skin material on an aluminium-honeycomb core. The latter was incorporated to provide a controlled crush resistance. It is interesting to note that while this design feature of a shock-absorbing nose box was desirable, at this stage it was not an obligatory requirement.

The side pods saw major change by being moulded from carbon pre-preg on Nomex honeycomb as total-sandwich components. These were hot cured under vacuum in female tooling, chosen to achieve the best finish on the outer face.

The one very interesting point to note is that despite the advances made in the use of modern composites, all models up to and including the FW09B, used wet-lay-up GRP for body panels and engine covers.

In 1985 there were again two variations from Williams: the FW10 and FW10B. Once more, geometric and aerodynamic changes caused the model change, but a major step was taken in the use of composites on both these

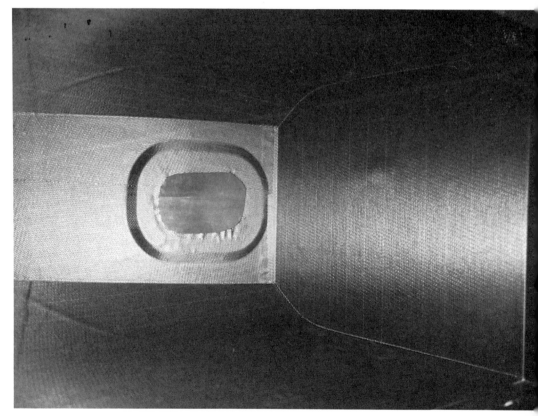

This and the following sequence of photographs show some of the stages in the lay-up of a Formula One monocoque by Williams GP Engineering. Shown here is the female mould with the first layer of woven carbon-fibre pre-preg in place

This close-up clearly shows the woven pre-preg accurately tailored around the fuel-tank bay

The monocoque mould with the Kevlar ply—which forms part of the outer skin laminate—in place

Below The first pre-preg laminated skin after its autoclave cure

variants. This was the design and construction of the first Williams carbon-fibre-and-honeycomb monocoque.

The method of manufacture consisted of the monocoque shell being made in female tooling, woven and UD carbon pre-pregs being applied in layers to achieve the desired skin thickness. This outer skin lamination was hot cured in the team's newly-acquired autoclave—this allowed a higher consolidating pressure during the cure—and a film adhesive was applied to the cured skin while it was still in the mould. The Nomex honeycomb and the inner skin were then hot cured in the autoclave as a second operation, producing the required sandwich structure. The monocoque floor and bulkheads were again carbon-skinned honeycomb components, which were assembled and bonded together using cold-set, two-part epoxy adhesive. The result was an extremely-successful monocoque and a manufacturing method that was to be used extensively.

The new cars were to see many advances being made, one being the now obligatory crush-resistant nose box. Further development of the use of aluminium honeycomb and carbon had resulted in this reaching the required performance. This model utilized carbon-skinned Nomex to form the undertray, with carbon pre-preg on aluminium honeycomb for the diffuser—the contoured air-flow extension of the undertray.

Another first was the use of laminated carbon pre-preg on honeycomb to form the engine cover which, again, was hot cured in female tooling. After a short period, the engine covers were remade, using the same method, but in Kevlar pre-preg instead of carbon. This produced a component of sufficient stiffness but which was lighter. Carbon pre-preg was also used to produce cooling ducts.

Right The monocoque after removal from the mould, having the inserts jig drilled

Below right The finished monocoque ready for final assembly into a complete car

Below This advanced stage of lay-up shows the honeycomb in place. Nomex honeycomb is used in the areas of more complex shape, as it is more flexible than aluminium honeycomb, which is employed on the flatter sides. Film adhesive is used between the honeycomb and the pre-cured outer skin. The load-bearing inserts, or hard points, can be seen in both types of honeycomb. After the pre-preg layers that form the inner skin have been put in place, a second autoclave cure completes the basic construction

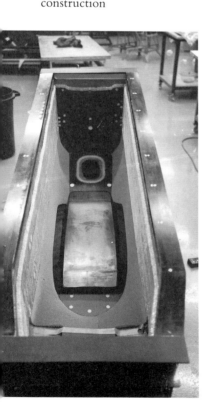

The completed Williams
FW10

Without doubt, the FW10/10B was a significant step by Williams in the design and utilization of modern composites.

The FW11 was built for 1986, and it utilized many of the previous model's production methods. These included the technique for producing the monocoque, which had a few additions. The first of these was a very significant step and concerned the driver-protection roll-hoop, which was formed as an integral part of the carbon monocoque. Further use of carbon-and-honeycomb sandwich on the monocoque included the suspension bulkhead, the seat-back and dash bulkheads (as used on the FW10). The nose-box assembly saw further developments. Although made of similar materials to that of the previous model, it now consisted of three components.

Modern composites were now being fully utilized, for, in addition to the previously-mentioned components, the FW11 boasted carbon radiator exit ducts and rear-wing mounting plates, again in laminated carbon. Laminated carbon pre-pregs were also used for assorted brackets.

If the FW11 was to be analysed by component, it would be clear that modern composites now form a major part of racing-car technology, but as this case history shows, Williams GP Engineering have and will, as long as they continue racing, push both racing-car design and the use of modern composites further ahead.

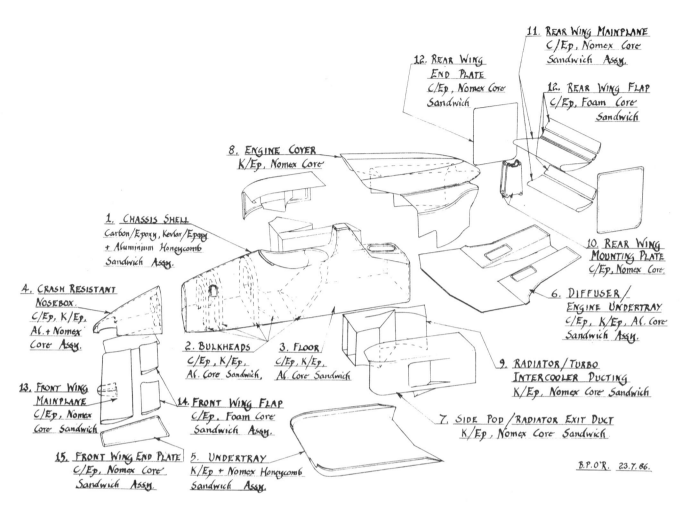

11. REAR WING MAINPLANE
C/Ep, Nomex Core
Sandwich Assy.

12. REAR WING
END PLATE
C/Ep, Nomex Core
Sandwich

12. REAR WING FLAP
C/Ep, Foam Core
Sandwich

8. ENGINE COVER
K/Ep, Nomex Core

1. CHASSIS SHELL
Carbon/Epoxy, Kevlar/Epoxy
+ Aluminium Honeycomb
Sandwich Assy.

4. CRASH RESISTANT
NOSEBOX.
C/Ep, K/Ep,
Al. + Nomex
Core Assy.

10. REAR WING
MOUNTING PLATE
C/Ep, Nomex Core

6. DIFFUSER /
ENGINE UNDERTRAY
C/Ep, K/Ep, Al. Core
Sandwich Assy.

2. BULKHEADS
C/Ep, K/Ep,
Al. Core Sandwich

3. FLOOR
C/Ep, K/Ep,
Al. Core Sandwich

9. RADIATOR/TURBO
INTERCOOLER DUCTING
K/Ep, Nomex Core Sandwich

13. FRONT WING
MAINPLANE
C/Ep, Nomex
Core Sandwich

14. FRONT WING FLAP
C/Ep, Foam Core
Sandwich Assy.

7. SIDE POD /RADIATOR EXIT DUCT
K/Ep, Nomex Core Sandwich

15. FRONT WING END PLATE
C/Ep, Nomex Core
Sandwich Assy.

5. UNDERTRAY
K/Ep + Nomex Honeycomb
Sandwich Assy.

B.P.O'R. 23.7.86.

Above The composite components that made up the Williams FW11

Right The 1980 Williams FW07B—a full ground-effect car that won both Constructors' and Drivers' World Championships

The race performance of Williams GP Engineering is legendary, and since the utilization of modern composites their successes include:

1979 (FW07) Five Grand Prix wins.
1980 (FW07B) Seven wins and both Constructors' and Drivers' World Championships.
1981 (FW07C) Five wins and Constructors' World Championship.
1982 (FW08) One win and Drivers' World Championship.
1983 (FW08C) One win.
1984 (FW09/09B) One win.
1985 (FW10) Four wins.
1986 (FW11) Nine wins and Constructors' World Championship.

This list of Grand Prix wins is a testimonial to both the designs of Patrick Head and the company leadership of Frank Williams.

The 1986 Williams FW11, winner of that season's Constructors' Championship with a remarkable nine Grand Prix wins

Part Three Composites in competition motorcycles

1 Summary
2 Armstrong Competition Motorcycles
3 Ducati
4 Honda
5 Gallina Suzuki
6 Heron Suzuki
7 A European composite motorcycle project
8 The Wheatley Lingham 500

1 Summary

With any advancing technology there will be both successes and failures, which are necessary to enforce progress. As previously mentioned, there have been bold attempts to utilize modern composites in racing-motorcycle design which have failed. These may have been due to too big a step being taken too quickly, owing to the pressure caused by the desire to be first with a new design, or the need to keep up with new technology and not having the know-how to meet the need, or perhaps just having the pioneering spirit (also necessary) which says 'Let's have a go.'

In the case of racing-motorcycle design, the pioneers have not had the advantage of a vast wealth of past composite chassis data to which they can refer, or a large number of composite users with whom they must keep abreast, as is the case with race cars.

Apart from the case histories of complete composite chassis designs, there are a considerable number of examples where composite components have been used for parts of motorcycles. In most cases, this will have been for some specific reason, such as added strength, weight saving or, sometimes, for ease of manufacture. Every one of these cases, even where only a comparatively small component is made in composite, shows that composite technology cannot be ignored, and there is always the very strong possibility that most of these small-scale users will develop the material's use.

Inevitably more teams will begin to make use of composites and, as in car racing, they will become the standard range of materials for the design and construction of racing motorcycles.

A well-known application for carbon fibre, which has been used quite widely by prominent motorcycle teams, is for brake discs and pads. Unlike other brake systems, where discs or drums are of a different material to the pad or shoe (i.e. a steel disc or drum with the pad or shoe in some non-metallic material), where carbon is used for brake discs, the pad is also made from the same material. For obvious reasons, this range of materials is not suitable for drum brakes.

When carbon fibres are used for brake components, the manufacturing processes are different. In most cases of carbon fibre use, binder resins are used, the structure or component being made by the mixture of fibres and resin. With brake components, no resin is used; the parts are formed by the use of extremely high pressure. Without this manufacturing process, carbon fibre could not be used for brake components, the reason being that available resin systems would not stand the extreme temperatures generated on the disc and pad surfaces. These can be as high as 600 degrees Celsius.

The advantages of using carbon fibre for brake components include reduced brake fade at the high temperatures generated, and a great saving in weight with reduced inertia. Most importantly, there is little or no distortion, even at the very high temperatures generated by braking. The apparent disadvantages seem to be few, but do include the fact that although carbon-fibre brakes resist fade at high temperatures, they do not offer good braking efficiency when cold. In racing this can be an important point, as long runs without braking can give them time to cool. Other disadvantages are the high wear rate, which is due to the disc and pad being made of the same material, and the fact that this type of brake is also very expensive in comparison to conventional brakes. In spite of these problems, the use of this type of brake is becoming standard on high-performance machines.

A particularly interesting use of carbon brake components was investigated by Automotive Products' Racing Division. This was a periferal brake disc, i.e. the carbon-fibre disc was of much larger diameter than normal. In fact, the disc was of the same diameter as the front wheel and was attached to the edge of the wheel rim instead of to the wheel centre, the aim being to increase brake surface area. This periferal disc was tested by the Heron Project 500 team on their composite Grand Prix machine and was raced in national events, but it was never used in a Grand Prix. Problems encountered during the development of this brake type may be overcome with further work, and this very interesting project may see the light of day again in the future.

A major area of notable success in the use of composites to improve a component in motorcycle racing is the use of carbon fibre to give additional stiffness to front forks. The main advantage this offers is improved resistance to bending under heavy braking, and distortion, or misalignment, due to side loading. It is interesting to note that this same result has been achieved by different teams using different methods of composite application as described below.

Yamaha utilized carbon fibre bonded to the inside of the fork legs as an integral part, as did Heron Suzuki. The latter employed unidirectional fibres for ultimate stiffness running down the length of the tube. The carbon pre-preg was placed on the inside of the fork leg, and then an inflatable sleeve was blown up in the centre to apply pressure to the pre-preg during the elevated-temperature cure cycle. This type of fork modification improved the fork-leg stiffness by a considerable amount.

A further development by Heron Suzuki was to improve the stiffness even more by placing the unidirectional carbon-fibre pre-preg on the outside of the fork tubes. This was achieved by putting the pre-preg in position and applying the required bonding pressure by the use of plastic shrink-wrap tape. This shrinks at elevated temperatures. The tape was wound around the fork tubes on top of the applied pre-preg, shrinking and applying pressure as the pre-preg was cured.

Another approach to the utilization of carbon fibre for stiffening front fork legs was made by Chevalier. They placed carbon fibre on the inside of the fork tubes, but the method of manufacture differed from the previously-described techniques. It consisted of curing the carbon-fibre pre-preg on some type of form, or mould, as a complete carbon component, and then, as a second stage, bonding it into the fork tubes. This method would allow total inspection of the carbon content, thus ensuring that the optimum performance was achieved from the composite. However, the clearance required to allow for assembly without displacing the adhesive, which is necessary to bond the carbon-fibre part into place, may be a disadvantage, as thick glue lines could be the weak link, if there is one.

In 1985 a very advanced step in the use of carbon fibre as a means of stiffening motorcycle front forks was taken by Honda, when they produced fork tubes entirely in carbon fibre instead of enhancing the performance of a pre-made metal component. This method of construction would allow the ultimate performance to be obtained from the type of carbon being used. It would also offer considerable weight saving. However, construction of this type of fork leg requires the best quality of workmanship in both tooling and handling of the composite, although it must be said that good workmanship is essential in all composite construction.

It is extremely difficult to compare the performance of forks modified by the use of composite materials, as those used by different teams differ in many ways—in design, materials etc—also general configurations will affect the forks' behaviour. Different riders may also have their own ideas about the feel produced by the forks.

It would appear that the use of composites can be a great aid to the modification of existing designs, in addition to their use for new totally-composite designs, but the composite type and method used will depend on the performance requirement, production facilities etc. Therefore, each case must be viewed with these points in mind.

One important point must be made in regard to the use of totally-composite front fork legs, and that is the safety factor. It has been proved that all-composite fork legs can work, but it must be pointed out that this type of structure will have virtually no fail-safe, i.e. the structure will either be complete and working as intended, or will have failed totally. Consequently, designs intended for this type of construction must be produced by persons with the right skills for this type of work. Modification, on the other hand, is only improving something which has already been proved to be safe.

Carbon fibre has been utilized in one very critical area concerning racing-motorcycle performance, and that is for fuel control valves in two-stroke engines. The material has been used for the valves in both disc-valve engines and reed-valve engines, different forms of carbon fibre being employed for two different reasons.

In the case of the disc valve, which, as its name implies, is a disc that revolves to expose and close the inlet ports, the use of carbon fibre serves to reduce weight and inertia. Another very important quality is that it does not suffer from the distortion problems associated with metallic discs. Discs for these valves are usually a multi-layer laminate of woven pre-preg, hot cured under positive pressure.

Reed valves differ in that they are almost static, i.e. they are formed as a flat sheet, or strip, which is fixed at one end, while the other is free and forms a flap which is lifted by pressure to expose the port. The reed, or flap, returns to close the port by virtue of its own stiffness. Carbon fibre is ideal for this application by virtue of its inherent stiffness. The use of unidirectional fibres running the length of the reed enables the designer to produce the required stiffness, which can be controlled by the fibre type or fibre thickness. One great advantage of using carbon is its resistance to softening, or taking on a set or bend, so that it retains its designed stiffness. Carbon fibre is becoming more widely used as a reed-valve material, and in some racing engines it is replacing the commonly-used glass-fibre reeds.

Composites have found many uses in the construction of racing motorcycles, for reasons other than structural performance, the main one being to save weight. One area where this can be achieved and composite technology can be used to good effect is in the manufacture of fairings.

Since the introduction of any form of streamlining on racing motorcycles, simple wet lay-up polyester and glass have been used, as previously described, because of the simplicity of manufacture and cheapness of both tooling, or moulds, and the fairings themselves. The materials now being used by some teams result in fairings that are much thinner and lighter, and in many cases stiffer, than before. These dramatic changes have been achieved by utilizing different resins and lighter and stronger fibres. One important step which has led to these much thinner laminates is the use of epoxy resin in place of polyester. This change of resin has been combined with the use of carbon, Kevlar, and improved, woven glass fibres.

In most cases, fairings will be laminated using more than one type of fibre. This mixture can be for technical requirements or reasons of cost. For example, it is common for fairing laminates to be layers of glass and carbon, the use of the latter serving to ensure stiffness but keep the laminate thin. Sometimes, the use of glass fibre layers is to prevent the laminate from being too stiff and, therefore, brittle. In other cases, the use of glass will be to keep down the cost. There are many possible combinations of these fibres, each user having a specific reason for their selection.

If the ultimate in weight saving is the aim, then Kevlar will be the selected material, but it will usually have a carbon-fibre border. This is to overcome the trimming problems associated with Kevlar. Carbon strips are also utilized on glass-laminated fairings, but in this case to enhance their stiffness rather than for trimming. Some fairings are made of a carbon-and-Kevlar hybrid, which is a fabric consisting of these two materials woven together. This type of material has a predetermined performance and, therefore, is somewhat restricting. When single-material weaves are used, the performance of the laminate can be adjusted by the use of more or less of the fibre type required.

All racing-motorcycle teams utilize composites in some form for fairings, but of those who use the latest modern composites, Yamaha have chosen carbon-Kevlar hybrid, as have Armstrong. Honda have used carbon fibre, while Suzuki have some all-glass fairings and some that are a mixture of carbon and glass, but the mixture was by individual layers of the different types. There are, of course, other teams who utilize similar materials and combinations for fairings.

Another interesting use of carbon fibre has been for silencers, the main reason being to save weight, but also to prevent the silencer from panting. It eliminates denting, too.

Yamaha have been successful in using unidirectional carbon for silencers, with the fibre direction around the barrel diameter. Armstrong have also tested silencers made from woven carbon fibre. Again, this is an area of composite use which may have been exploited by many more teams.

Many small components used on racing motorcycles have been made from composites, mainly for weight reduction or to get the same strength from a much smaller component. These include such things as carbon footrest plates. Heron Suzuki have used a thick carbon laminate to manufacture front-fork bracers, and have also used carbon-fibre-laminated sprocket spacers, and seat supports and various other brackets to mount rev counters etc in composite sandwich materials. In most cases, these parts utilized carbon fibres as a means of saving weight and, in certain cases, for ease of manufacture, the strength requirement always being the prime consideration.

One idea, which has been attempted, and even raced (with poor results), is the use of composites for racing wheels. The weight saving and stiffness advantages are obvious, but the nature of this primary structure seems to have retarded the development of composites for this purpose. However, as confidence and expertise grow, wheels are an area of motorcycle construction which will eventually make full use of modern composites.

When all the component types, large and small, are considered, together with all the manufacturers using modern composites, it shows that, apart from the major chassis projects, wider use of these materials is being made. Where smaller, or non-structural components are being made, they serve to give confidence and allow steady progress into a new technology for each new user.

Motorcycle racing is making steady progress in the utilization of modern composites, and this can only be good for both the sport and the technology. This has got to lead to an exciting and progressive future.

2 Armstrong Competition Motorcycles

In 1983 Armstrong Competition Motorcycles took a giant step forward in racing-motorcycle chassis design by producing a machine with structural dependence on modern composites. The carbon-fibre-skinned, honeycomb-sandwich construction was designed and built to house a Rotax 250 cc engine, and exactly the same chassis also raced with an Armstrong-manufactured 350 cc engine. This was to be the first known motorcycle chassis made completely in composite, including the rear swinging fork.

The two components of the chassis, that is the main frame and the swinging fork, were both made in female tooling. Laminated, woven carbon fibre was utilized as a skin material on aluminium honeycomb, the cure being completely carried out by the use of the vacuum method. To achieve the designed configuration, the components were made by the two-shot method.

One very significant point on this chassis design was that all the inserts and load-bearing hard points were pre-made and then bonded, or moulded, in during the manufacturing process. The end result had a very clean and smooth outer finish, while still meeting the structural requirements.

The Armstrong has been an outstanding racing-motorcycle chassis, as demonstrated by the fact that exactly the same design has been used for three different engine sizes, or formulae, and, having met the design requirements, has remained unchanged for three years of racing. In fact, at the time of writing, the first chassis was still in competition.

This advanced and exciting use of composites is a credit to designer Mike Eatough, and to Paul Owens who supplied the composite technology.

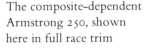

The composite-dependent Armstrong 250, shown here in full race trim

Right and below right Two views showing the general layout of the carbon-fibre chassis and swinging rear fork of the very advanced Armstrong machine

Bottom right The Armstrong's very light and stiff chassis being put to the test

Below This view of the Armstrong clearly shows the moulded-carbon-fibre, split-backbone chassis

3 Ducati

The Ducati composite chassis, showing the use of rivets as a method of joining the flat panels. The machined metal structures housing the steering-head bearing and the various pivot points can also be seen

In recent years many racing motorcycles have made use of modern composites for small individual components, usually for some significant reason, and such use of composites can generate greater confidence in the materials and lead to their use for larger and structurally-dependent parts. With motorcycles, however, this has not been the case. It is an accepted fact that competition-motorcycle designs utilizing modern composites are several years behind their counterparts in the motor-racing world—with one notable exception.

As early as 1980, Ducati had engaged the services of Italian designer Luigi

In this view of the Ducati chassis, the make-up of the alloy-honeycomb, sandwich-panel side members can be seen at the seat extension and the small apertures in the top and side panels. Note the use of honeycomb sandwich as the lower front-fork bracer. The horizontal bulkhead forming the fuel-tank base is also alloy-honeycomb sandwich and is a structural part of the chassis

Segale to design a chassis for the TTF2 class. The resulting design was to be an exciting step forward for motorcycle design because of its use of modern composites in a fully structural manner. The revolutionary design utilized aluminium honeycomb sandwiched between alloy skins, resulting in very light and stiff panels. These were purchased in flat, pre-made form, and the chassis was fabricated from them.

The unique chassis layout consisted of two flat, vertical side members, separated by a horizontal bulkhead, or panel, which served as both a structural component and the seat base. This bulkhead extended forward, dropping down between the side members, but over the engine to leave a cavity above the bulkhead and between the side members to form the fuel cell. In other words, the fuel tank became an integral part of the chassis. The method used to join the side members to the bulkhead comprised an alloy angle capping with a double row of rivets through each face.

The steering head was a machined, solid-alloy, subframe-like structure, housing the steering-head bearings. It was attached to the honeycomb-

sandwich side members by allowing the sandwich skins to overlap the subframe and then fixing them with a double row of rivets. All the other main structural mounting points, such as the pivot for the magnesium swinging fork and the top mountings for the twin rear dampers, were also machined components which were placed in the edges of the sandwich side members and retained by double rows of rivets.

Two thicknesses of sandwich panels were used in this design, the horizontal bulkhead being much thinner than the vertical side members. This saved both weight and space where design would allow. The resulting chassis was a box-like structure, open at the bottom to contain the engine.

One other interesting application for honeycomb sandwich in this design was the lowest of the three front fork bracers. This was a flat, shaped piece that was of a similar material to that used for the horizontal bulkhead. In fact, this bracer served a similar function to that of a small bulkhead.

The Ducati chassis would appear to be ahead of its time, both from technical and appearance standpoints. Similar materials have been used since and, apart from the use of rivets, it could have been mistaken for a current development. However, modern techniques would have led to the use of adhesive on the joint areas. Not only does this give greater shear strength, but it also eliminates the problems associated with riveted joints.

It is sad to report that, apart from some spasmodic testing, this excellent development was not allowed to show its potential. The company chose instead to race a more traditional chassis, which was being developed at the same time. This was possibly a great loss to motorcycle racing, as it appears to have been the first full monocoque motorcycle chassis designed and built from modern composites.

4 Honda

This photograph shows the skeletal appearance of the Honda NR 500 chassis. Note the use of metallic fasteners for joining the various parts of the chassis together. The machined, metal steering-head bearing housing and swinging-rear-fork pivot points can be clearly seen. Other significant carbon-fibre components shown include the rear swinging fork, the wheels and the silencer

Although already a current world contender in Grand Prix motorcycle racing, with well established and very competitive machinery, in 1984 Honda were to support a very far-sighted approach and take a big step forward by fielding a totally new design of chassis based on the use of modern composite materials. This was the NR 500, which was to be powered by the current V4 engine.

Almost without doubt, for a prototype, the NR 500 used more component parts in carbon fibre than any other known composite bike project. This bold advance in technology illustrates the effect composites have on design and why Honda have been such a formidable force in this very competitive sport.

The chassis of the Honda NR 500 demonstrated a very different approach to the use of carbon fibre than any other motorcycle design. It was of skeletal construction, the components being comparatively narrow in

section, resulting in a low-mass, open, frame-like structure. The parts of this chassis utilized woven carbon fibre which was formed by moulding, the component thickness being achieved by using additional carbon layers to form a multi-layer laminate. This laminate thickness and the shape were calculated to give the required performance—no honeycomb was used. Moulding of the chassis parts utilized pre-preg, which was cured at elevated temperature, using vacuum to achieve the required bonding pressure.

The various chassis sections were mechanically joined, using metallic fastenings, similar to aircraft methods. At major stress points—the steering head and the swinging-rear-fork mounting—machined metallic components were used. These were attached to the chassis structure with metallic fastenings.

There are no reported torsional or bending stiffness figures for the Honda chassis, so its performance cannot be assessed. Furthermore, apart from some testing, very little has been seen of it, and no further development of this very interesting and different approach to the utilization of modern composites has appeared.

Carbon fibre was also used to produce the swinging rear fork of the NR500. Again, moulding in female tools was the method of manufacture and, as with the chassis, machined metal inserts were used for bearing or load-bearing points and were moulded in. The rear-wheel spindle mounting was also metallic.

The wheels of the NR500 also displayed a very advanced and very different use of resin-reinforced carbon fibre, the component parts being made and joined mechanically with metallic fastenings. Each wheel comprised the rim and spoke plates.

The wheel rim was made using a multi-layer laminate which consisted of eight layers of woven carbon-fibre pre-preg. This had a higher curing temperature than normal to achieve the best possible performance. Bonding pressure was by press in matched tools to achieve an accurate surface shape on both sides of the component. The finished rim shape was conventional, with a vertical flange around the inner centre of the rim. This flange formed the mounting point for the outer ends of the spokes.

The spoke plates were also press cured in matched tooling to achieve consistency of thickness and surface finish on both faces. Unlike the rims, the spoke plates were made mainly with unidirectional carbon-fibre pre-preg, running in line with the spoke direction. Some woven pre-preg was placed in the centre and on the two outer surfaces of the resultant multi-layer laminate to prevent longitudinal splitting of the spoke, or fibre separation due to most of the fibres being straight and laying in one direction. The use of unidirectional fibres was to optimize the fibre performance where most needed. Also, the shape of these spoke plates was ideal for this form of laminate.

The two spoke plates were fixed to the metallic hub centre and to the rim flange with metallic fastenings.

The drilling of holes in the carbon-fibre spoke plates may have been the cause of one reported rear-wheel failure. In photographs it did appear that

An excellent example of moulded carbon-fibre pre-preg. Matched moulds were used to produce the component parts of this Honda wheel. The carbon spoke plates and rim are bolted to the metallic hub centre. Note the constant laminate thickness of the sectioned rim sample

failure was in the region of the spoke-plate/rim attachment, but this has not been confirmed. It would appear that additional strength could have been achieved if the spoke had been made wider at the point of drilling. This would have made allowance for carbon fibre lost due to the holes.

This very advanced wheel design has shown to what extent modern composites can be utilized. Further development and use would be very good for Honda, motorcycle racing, and composite technology in general.

Another very significant step in the advance of composite technology was the use of carbon fibre for the front fork tubes of the NR 500. Carbon fibre has been used in several ways to improve the stiffness of metallic fork tubes, but Honda produced tubes that were totally composite in structure. The material chosen for the front fork tubes was unidirectional carbon fibres, and the method of manufacture consisted of these fibres being filament wound on to a mandrel. The fibres were helically wound at opposing angles to the direction of the mould, and in the case of the Honda tubes, these angles were ± 20 degrees. Tubes made in carbon by this method produce the ideal basis for forks, because they have greater flexural rigidity than metallic tubes of the same proportions.

Internal slideability and sealability are achieved by one of two methods. One is to apply a thin coat of metal to the inner surface by a plating process, and the other is to coat the surface with a layer of resin. Both methods are claimed to provide slideability and sealability equal to, if not better than, normal metallic fork legs.

Although the fork tubes are now at a usable level of development, there are still some disadvantages to be overcome. The tubes' circular and torsional rigidity are both, at this time, inferior to steel tubes, and they suffer from exterior erosion caused by flying stones etc. However, the advantage of the greater stiffness, coupled with reduced mass, makes further development worthwhile.

The NR 500 contained a vast amount of composite technology, which shows great progress for both Honda and motorcycle racing in general. These advances will almost certainly lead to yet more development and further progress to widen the use and potential of modern composites.

This photograph shows the superb finish on more Honda components: a swinging rear fork, a front tube, a wheel, and front and rear carbon brake discs and pads

5 Gallina Suzuki

During the 1983–84 season, while the British Heron Suzuki Project 500 was underway, their Italian counterparts were also taking steps to utilize modern composites in an effort to improve on the current, standard alloy chassis. The new design, by Robert Gallina, was intended to house the XR70 square-four GP engine in current use and was known as the TG1A. This experimental design had the appearance of a deep-section, split-backbone-type layout.

The method of construction consisted of deep channel-section chassis side members being made in aluminium alloy, and then honeycomb was placed strategically into the channel, which was enclosed by the addition of a fourth side. Carbon fibre was used as an extra reinforcement on this fourth side. This produced a box-like structure with honeycomb as the core material.

The TG1A did appear at test sessions, but was never run in a Grand Prix. It is reported that it was later sold to a private buyer and was used in European racing. The reason for the design not being used, or developed further, has not been disclosed, but it could be due to one or many factors not associated with the use of composites.

It is important to note that a sandwich structure in composite materials may produce a very stiff, strong construction, but how this is integrated into the chassis, or the basic chassis layout, can affect the overall chassis performance. In some cases the chassis may be as intended but not utilized for other reasons.

6 Heron Suzuki

When Suzuki withdrew from Grand Prix racing in 1983, the Heron Corporation in Great Britain were able to acquire the XR40 square-four engines. A decision to produce a new design for these engines resulted in Nigel Leaper being engaged as designer, and an investigation into the possible use of modern composites resulted in the Heron Project 500.

As the Project 500 had been designed for composite use, the new chassis was completely different in appearance to conventional frames, or variants of conventional designs. It was a box-like structure, which housed the small square-four engine.

After a detailed study of the relevant composites and methods of use, Nigel Leaper decided to design for a fabricated method rather than a moulded form. It was considered that to fabricate from pre-made panels eliminated the need for expensive mould tools but, more important, that changes could easily be made during the prototype stage.

The material from which the chassis was to be constructed was pre-made, aluminium-skinned, aluminium honeycomb. As in most cases, the skin type, thickness etc, and honeycomb type, were selected by calculating the final panel performance, using the performance details of the individual materials. The actual fabrication was by the previously-described cut-and-fold method, in the same fashion as the earlier all-aluminium-honeycomb race-car chassis.

Heron Suzuki's first Project 500 model, showing the composite chassis, which was made from aluminium-skinned, aluminium honeycomb. The chassis was fabricated from pre-made flat panels. Note the experimental composite front disc brake that was attached to the wheel rim rather than the hub

The XR70 carbon-fibre-skinned, aluminium honeycomb chassis was similar in layout to the previous XR45 all-aluminium model, but was lighter and stiffer

The resultant chassis design showed a very significant improvement in both bending and torsional stiffness. This improved stiffness was to give the machine excellent handling qualities and made it more responsive to race settings.

During early testing and the first season's racing, the chassis proved to be almost indestructable, having suffered from being dropped several times at speeds well in excess of 100 mph. In one particular case, the bike rolled at high speed, resulting in almost everything being destroyed, with the exception of the chassis and the engine. The same machine raced again in a very short time.

This very new and revolutionary design was race ready for the last three Grand Prix of the 1984 season, and was to achieve seventh, fifth and sixth placings, giving the rider, Rob McElnea, eleventh place in the World Championship.

For the 1985 season, chassis development was taken further by the use of carbon-fibre pre-preg. The chassis layout was similar to the 1984 version, the difference being that the pre-made panel from which the chassis was fabricated had laminated skins. These were still of aluminium, but of thinner gauge and with unidirectional carbon pre-preg laminated to the outer faces. The resultant panel enabled the chassis to be fabricated in a similar fashion as before, but it produced even greater stiffness and a very important reduction in weight.

The new model was to use the XR45 engine, which was an uprated version of the ageing square-four design. Ridden by Rob McElnea, it was to perform well, considering its lack of horsepower. Its more notable placings in Grand Prix events were two fifth places, a seventh and a sixth, resulting in the rider obtaining ninth place in the World Championship.

In 1986 Heron Suzuki machines were to utilize the XR70 engine, which was yet another version of the square-four, the most significant difference

Right The very stiff carbon chassis of the XR70 being put to the test

Right and below right Two views of the composite-dependent Heron Suzuki 500 cc XR70 during the 1986 GP season

Above The third composite
chassis design from Heron
Suzuki, which was
constructed from pre-
made, flat, carbon-fibre-
skinned, honeycomb-
sandwich panels. This
unique chassis was built to
house the XR71 V4 engine,
which replaced the
previous square-four
engine

Above left The classic lines
of the Heron Suzuki 500 cc
GP contender are obvious
in this action shot. The
fabricated carbon-fibre and
honeycomb chassis is
different in appearance to a
conventional tubular
chassis

Left From the front, the
small overall size of the
Heron Suzuki XR70 is
obvious

being the use of reed valves instead of disc valves. This change was claimed
to improve the horsepower delivered by the now very dated engine design.

The new machine was to be ridden by another rider, Rob McElnea
having been courted by another team, and the season did not yield much
success until the last three Grand Prix, when an extra machine was raced
by Neil MacKensie. This resulted in two sevenths and an eighth place,
giving the rider tenth place in the World Championship. This was the first
time he had raced 500 cc machines.

Suzuki then made a positive move towards supporting Grand Prix
racing by producing a brand-new engine design. In keeping with current
competitive engines from other factories, this was in the form of a V4. The
engine was to be used by Heron in an entirely new design of chassis for the
1987 season.

The 1987 design still utilized honeycomb sandwich structures as the basis,
but the layout was changed to suit the different engine shape. The side
elevation shows a much smaller section, but to achieve the required performance, the panel thickness was increased; that is the skins of the panel
are further apart. Also the skins were made completely of UD carbon fibre.
This was another forward step that further increased the chassis stiffness
with a reduction in weight.

Unfortunately, before the new design could be tried in competition,
Suzuki took over direct responsibility for their Grand Prix road-racing
effort once more and switched back to a Japanese-designed, conventional
aluminium chassis.

7 A European composite motorcycle project

Another attempt to utilize composites in the manufacture of a racing-motorcycle chassis was carried out in Germany. It would appear that the aim was to save weight rather than to enhance stiffness, and there are no recorded torsional or bending stiffness figures for the design. The chassis was designed to accommodate the Rotax 250, and presumably it was intended to contest that formula. This very unique design employed honey-comb-sandwich panels, and all the composite parts were cut from pre-made flat panels.

In appearance, the chassis layout was of a back-bone type, with a flat top and sides. These sandwich-panel parts were linked by a collection of magnesium castings, one carrying the steering head, and one on each side to the rear of the engine which held the side members and served as mounting points for the rear suspension.

The rear suspension was designed as a parallelogram; that is two swinging forks in parallel. These two fork members consisted of five pieces of sandwich panel cut to the rear-fork shape to accept the rear wheel, then stacked to give the required depth. Again, these pieces were linked at both ends with magnesium castings, with two further castings linking the two fork members and carrying the rear spindle. All the component parts were then simply bonded together.

Unfortunately, there is no documented evidence of the outcome of this interesting and different approach to the use of composites.

8 The Wheatley Lingham 500

This case history of a racing-motorcycle design proves that the utilization of modern composites is not restricted to works and heavily-sponsored teams. The design was conceived and financed entirely as a private venture.

Gary Lingham, a successful amateur motorcycle racer since 1977, met Chris Wheatley in 1985 and together they decided to utilize the latter's knowledge of carbon fibre to produce a composite chassis for racing in the 500 cc class during 1986. The proposed design was to house an RG500 engine and consisted of a carbon-fibre-based chassis, the same materials being used to produce the rear swinging fork. The component parts were produced by the moulded method.

The technique used to produce the moulded chassis began with making full-size patterns in wood from prepared drawings. Split GRP moulds were formed from the wooden patterns. These moulds were made from epoxy-reinforced glass, the splits being a means of mould separation to facilitate the removal of the component after completion of the moulding or laminating process.

The Wheatley Lingham 500 in full race trim

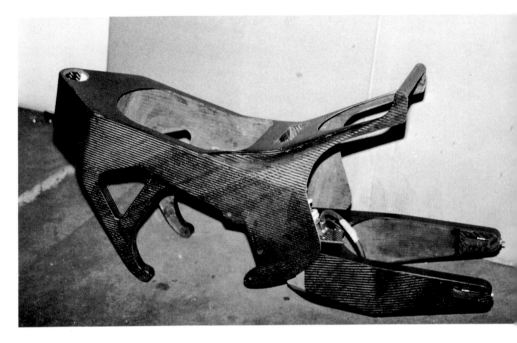

The moulded carbon-fibre chassis and swinging fork of the Wheatley Lingham 500, which are probably the most advanced use of composites in motorcycle racing by a privately-sponsored team

One very significant step taken in the construction of this chassis was that it was moulded in one piece from woven carbon-fibre skins on aluminium honeycomb, resulting in a very stiff sandwich structure. This form of construction is carried out by tailoring the selected carbon-fibre pre-preg into the mould, the skin thickness being controlled by the number of layers used. The aluminium honeycomb is then shaped and placed in the mould, followed by more carbon-fibre layers to form the second skin. Next, the pre-preg is cured at an elevated temperature, and pressure to consolidate this assembly during the cure is applied by means of vacuum, as described earlier.

Other additions to this chassis included an aluminium insert moulded in at the steering-head junction to carry the head bearings. Where mountings had to be attached to the chassis or bolts passed through, extra support was provided by moulding in solid-carbon inserts. The rear swinging fork was of similar construction to the chassis, but was manufactured in two halves and then bonded together as a second operation.

The complete composite chassis with rear swinging fork weighed 8 kg and was considered to be over-engineered, but as there are no documented torsional and bending stiffness figures, this point cannot be substantiated.

Lack of finance prevented this private venture from having an engine that was good enough to fully test the interesting design under racing conditions. However, at the 1986 British Grand Prix Gary Lingham was in a very creditable seventh place in the wet until he was robbed again by another engine failure on the twenty-third lap out of 28.

This machine has since been passed on to a new owner in Ireland, where it appears to make the top few places in races on the local circuits.

With the right support, this very bold private attempt to fully utilize modern composites may have been a real success story.

Part Four Postscript

1 Composite structure safety
2 Conclusion

1 Composite structure safety

Much has been said about the stiffness etc of composite race-car structures from the performance aspect, but of greater importance, especially to the driver, is their performance in a crash. As described previously, modern composites (in the form of pre-pregs) can be utilized to meet a strength or stiffness requirement by the strategic arrangement of fibre direction. This same feature can be used to offer additional protection. Earlier metallic structures did not have this versatility, and extra structural performance, or protection, usually meant an increase in weight.

The best illustration of these points has come about since the introduction in 1985 of the frontal crash requirement for Formula One cars, which requires a mass of 750 kg (this represents a full car) to be impacted from 32 mph (51.49 km/h). Resultant damage must not reach the driver's foot area, or cause movement of the pedals. Almost without exception, this test has been passed by the designer's clever use of modern fibre technology and honeycomb.

One outstanding feature of metallic honeycomb is its unique shock-absorbing properties. If this material is loaded in the direction of the cells, that is similar to applying pressure to the ends of a tube, a high initial resistance, or strength, prevails. If the load increases, the cell walls begin to buckle, each cell or tube beginning to concertina. The load required to cause continuation of cell-wall buckling, although lower than the initial load, then remains constant. From the shock-absorbing aspect, this phenomenon is similar, whatever the rate of load. In the impact situation, the initial high strength reduces impact speed, and the following constant crush resistance serves as the vital energy absorber.

Several factors control both the initial strength peak and constant crush resistance of honeycomb: the cell size, the material from which the honeycomb is made, and the cell-wall thickness. These material permutations enable the designer to achieve the required performance with the minimum of added weight. In addition to their shock-absorbing qualities, modern composite chassis can be designed to have excellent penetration resistance, which is another important point where driver protection is concerned.

One very significant point has emerged on the crash performance of the modern composite chassis, which utilizes a fibre-skinned, honeycomb-sandwich-type structure, and that is that impact damage remains very localized. This damage restriction is due to the widely-used carbon-fibre skins having virtually no elastic limit; that is a point where deformation due to load becomes permanent, as would be the case with an aluminium monocoque. The same applies to a tubular-steel construction. In both cases, if sufficient load deforms the structure beyond its elastic limit, then the

The crushing effect of a frontal impact was halted by the honeycomb-sandwich panels surrounding the side mounted fuel cells of this car, probably saving the driver's life. This early use of composites was to lead to a much expanded use of structural sandwich, which is illustrated throughout this book

deformation becomes permanent. This results in the structure, or chassis, remaining in one piece but collapsing until the energy has been absorbed. The carbon-fibre chassis, with its immense stiffness, does not deform in the same way. The stiffness serves to transmit the load further into the structure, which means that higher loads can be absorbed without permanent damage to the structure.

In the case of the carbon structure, if the load exceeds the absolute strength of the laminate, then failure is total. This is the reason for adding a laminate of Kevlar, to act as a fail-safe.

The use of Kevlar as a fail-safe is not universal. In fact, more chassis are now produced without it, than with. This is due to experience gained through test work and racing accidents. Experience, coupled with almost unlimited performance capability, allows the modern designer to produce a monocoque, or chassis, with such a level of stiffness and strength that the fail-safe aspect is no longer a major consideration.

In many cases, there is another reason for the exclusion of Kevlar from primary structures of carbon, and that is the previously-mentioned inter-laminar shear problems associated with its use. If the fail-safe layer of Kevlar could be the outer layer of the laminate, this would minimize some of the problems. However, although this would make it ideal for penetration protection, for obvious reasons, in this position, it would be unsuitable as a fail-safe.

Due to the versatility of modern composites, designers have, and will, continue to produce working designs, which differ in layout and choice of materials, to achieve the same end result. Furthermore, in some cases, they will contradict the theories of others.

All these points are what have made the use of modern composites in the areas covered by this book so exciting and technically interesting. There is little doubt that as more composite suppliers strive to glean business by advancing the technical capabilities of their products, designers will continue to utilize these advances. Based on this, modern composites, and competition cars and motorcycles, have a very exciting future.

The structural performance achieved by the use of modern composites and the resultant driver protection have been demonstrated to all race fans over the last few seasons by the apparently horrific crashes from which drivers have walked away. In many cases, this is due to the now exclusively-used carbon-fibre monocoque being strong enough not to disintegrate and, most importantly, being non-deformable, thus preventing the driver from being crushed.

Motor racing always has been, and always will be, dangerous, but modern composites have given designers the opportunity to make competition cars safer for the driver than was possible with previously-used, traditional materials in all their forms. The quest for performance will ensure that designers demand more and more from composite technology, and this, in turn, will lead to even greater safety.

2 Conclusion

The author showing his confidence in the technology he has spent over ten years recommending and selling to competition-vehicle designers and builders. Lola Cars invited him to accompany Guy Edwards on some laps of the Silverstone circuit in the composite-dependent Lola 610. A few laps on wet tyres, at a record lap average of 111.89 mph, were enough to convince the author of the exacting performance demanded of both driver and car

The range of modern composites, as covered by this book, has been developed by use in many industries, but the use in competition cars— formula racing cars in particular—has, without doubt, caused a greater advance in composite technology than any other, outside the aircraft industry. Indeed, it is claimed by some to have designers and technicians who are second to none in composite technology.

In the motorcycle world, the designers who have opted for modern composites in a structural form have been far fewer in number, and have had no advantage of established techniques. This may be due to their generally much smaller budgets, but as this book shows, those who have based designs on composites have proved their technical advantages, which will certainly lead to wider use and, one day, almost universal application, as in the race-car world.

Other industries will utilize modern composites, and the future of this technology is certain to be as progressive over the next ten years as it has been over the last ten. The teams, designers and technicians discussed in the book will almost certainly be major contributors.

Index

A

adhesives
  epoxy 18, 46, 73, 78, 90
  film 17, 20, 26, 34, 39, 42, 66, 71, 75, 86
    high performance 14
    phenol-based 10
    phenolic 17, 18, 52
    structural 18
    synthetic resin 42
    two-component 17
aerodynamic structure 60
Aeroweb 42
air-bleed mat 31
air-cooling ducts 83
Alfa Romeo 41
aluminium honeycomb 14
Aramid fibre 22
Armstrong Competition
    Motorcycles 100, 101, 102–103
ATS 41
attachment points 29
autoclave 25, 26, 30, 34, 35, 46, 55, 60, 78, 82, 90
Automotive Products 98

B

balanced laminates 30
Baldwin, John 40
balsa 75
Barclay Arrows 40
Barnard, John 75, 77
Benetton Formula 46–51
binder resins 97
Bluebird 42
bonding pressure 25, 34
body panels 23, 29, 30, 71
Bolster, John 16
Brabham 81–83
brake discs and pads (motorcycle) 97
buck 13
bulkheads 42, 46, 61, 72, 83, 90, 105
Burns, Rory 46, 51

C

Campbell, Donald 42
carbon fibre 21, 27, 29, 39, 46, 54, 59,
61, 66, 71, 77, 81, 86, 87, 97, 102, 107, 110, 112, 117, 121
CART series 39, 40, 66, 73, 84
caul plate 26, 35
Chaparral 39
chassis 26, 27, 30, 34, 39, 40, 42, 61
  carbon 41, 74
  race-car 36, 71
  wooden 16
Chevalier 98
CIBA (ARL) 44
Cobb, John 42
cold curing 17, 19
cold-set polyesters 13
cold-set resin systems 25
Cooper 52–53
Coppuck, Gordon 75
crash performance 121
crush resistance 88, 121
cure
  cycle 25, 27, 30, 32, 35, 62, 72, 98
  temperature 17, 19, 20, 27, 34, 78
  time 27
  two-stage 34
cut-and-fold method 36, 54, 72, 111

D

Data General Team Tyrrell 41
De Bruyne, Dr 14
De Havilland Aircraft Company 14
Design Council 62
disc valve 99
drapability (fibre) 21, 29
driver protection 123
Ducati 104–106
ducting 13, 23, 26, 30, 62, 77, 90

E

Eatough, Mike 102
Ecclestone, Bernie 83
engine
  air intakes 83
  cover 56
  inlet plenum 47
  mountings 46, 72
epoxy adhesive 18, 46, 73, 78, 90
epoxy resin 18, 21, 100
  shelf life 19

epoxy tooling resins 27
exotherm 19

F

fail-safe 23, 24, 55, 99, 122
fairings 13, 23, 30, 100
Ferrari 54–58
  126/C2 54
  126/C3 55
fibre distortion 21, 26
fibreglass 13
fibre pre-impregnation 19, 20
fibre range 20
film adhesives 17, 20, 26, 34, 39, 46, 66, 71, 75, 86
Fittipaldi 39
foaming resin system 29
footrest plates 101
Ford 59–60
Formula One 40, 46, 52, 54, 66, 71, 75, 81, 84, 87, 121
Formula Two 46, 66
Formula Three 84
Formula 3000 70
front forks 98, 109
  bracers 101, 106
fuel cells 39, 82, 88, 105
fuel control valves 99

G

Gallina, Robert 110
Gallina Suzuki 110
  TG1A 110
glass fibre 13, 22, 54, 59, 71, 75, 100
  pre-impregnated 23
glass-reinforced plastic 13
Glass Transition 27
Gordon Aerolight 10
ground-contact skirts 81
ground-effect cars 47, 73, 76
Group C 61, 66
GRP 13, 14, 16, 17, 39, 46, 52, 66, 88

H

Haas, Carl 40
hardener 13
Head, Patrick 94
Henderson, Phil 51
Hercules 77

Herd, Robin 40, 75
Heron Corporation 111
Heron Suzuki 98, 110, 111–115
    Project 500 98, 110, 111
Hesketh 54
Hidux 42
Honda 99, 100, 107–109
    NR 500 107
honeycomb 14, 18, 19, 29, 34, 39, 46,
        61, 81, 86, 110, 121
    aluminium 14, 42, 52, 66, 71, 87,
        102, 105, 111, 118
    core density 16
    core thickness 16
    first structural use 39
    non-metallic 29
    sandwich boards 35
hot-air blower 28
hot curing 17
hot-wire method 83, 87
Hunt, James 75
hybrid material 62, 71, 100

I
IMSA 65, 66
Indianapolis 40, 66, 73
inserts 29, 42, 46, 54, 72, 76, 102, 108,
        118
    potted 78
inter-laminar shear failure 23, 122

J
Jaguar 61–65
    XJR-6 61
    XJR-8, XJR-9 65
    XJS 61

K
Kevlar 21, 39, 47, 55, 59, 61, 69, 71,
        82, 86, 90, 100, 122

L
lay-up 27, 28, 34, 35, 55, 71, 78
    wet 27
Leaper, Nigel 111
Ligier 40
Lingham, Gary 117
Lola Cars 66–70
    T850, T600, T610 66
    T700, T800, T810, T900 69
    T86/50 70
Lola Ford 40
Lotus 79 71
Lotus Cars 39
louvre panels 48
low-vacuum technique 34

M
MacKensie, Neil 115
Maddock, Owen 52
March Engineering 40
matrix resins 21
    polyester 13
McElnea, Rob 112
McLaren 75–80
    M23, M26, M28 75
    M29, M30 76
    Malite car 75
    MP4 77
metal-to-metal bonding 10, 17
Minardi 41
monocoque 46, 54, 66, 71, 75, 81, 84,
        87, 122
    aluminium 39, 80, 121
    carbon-and-honeycomb 40
Motor Panels Ltd 44
Motor Racing Developments
        (Brabham) 81–83
    BT48, BT49C, BT50, BT52 81
    BT53, BT54, BT55 83
mould-making resin 27
moulds 10, 13, 25, 26, 27, 31, 35,
    split GRP 117
    female 28
Murray, Gordon 83

N
National Motor Museum 44
node bond 14
Nomex 29, 46, 59, 62, 66, 82, 87
Norris Bros 42
nose box 47, 62, 88
nose cone 56
nose splitter 66

O
Oatley, Neil 40
one-shot method 66
Osella 41
oven 25, 30, 35, 72
    hot-air circulating 32
Owens, Paul 102

P
peel srength 18
penetration resistance 121
Penske, Roger 40
phenol-based adhesives 10
phenolic adhesive 17, 18, 52
phenolic resin 10
    systems 17, 18, 22
Piquet, Nelson 83
platen press 25, 35, 42
polyamide foam 46

polyester resin 13, 27
    systems 17
polymer cross-linking 17, 20
polystyrene foam 75
post cure 19, 27
Postlethwaite, Dr Harvey 54
pre-pregs 19, 20, 22, 26, 28
    adhesive 21
    laminating 21
    performance 22
    uni-directional (UD) 20, 26, 98
process methods 25
Project Four Ltd 77

R
racing wheels (motorcycle) 101, 108
Ram 41
random-fibre mat 13
rear swinging fork 102, 108, 117
rear wing 66, 83, 86, 87
    end plates 46, 54, 87
    mounting pylon 46, 66
Redux 42
reed valves 99
release agent 13, 28, 35
    wax 28
release film 31
Renault 41
resin
    epoxy 18, 21
    foaming 29
    phenolic 10, 17, 22
    polyester 13, 17
    pre-impregnation 20
resin-filled fibre 20
resin-to-fibre ratio 20
Reynard Racing 84–86
roll hoop 49, 92

S
safety 121–123
sandwich structure 18, 21, 25, 29, 30,
        34, 36, 39, 46, 54, 59, 66, 72, 75,
        82, 86, 87, 110, 115, 118
    all-metal 39
Segale, Luigi 104
shear strength 18
Shell mileage marathon 59
shrink-wrap tape 98
side fences 46
side pods 39, 40, 69, 73, 75, 87
side skirts 76
silencers (motorcycle) 101
single-part resin system 19
Southgate, Tony 61
space-frame 54, 71
Spirit 39

sprocket spacers 101
structural adhesives 18
surface table 25
suspension 58, 72
Suzuki 100, 111, 115

T
tack bolts 78
Team Haas 40
Team Lotus 71–74
templates 28
thermal stress 30
thermocouple
   temperature recording 32
thermo setting 17, 19, 20, 25, 27
Toleman
   Group Motorsport 46
   TG181, TG182, TG183(A) 46
   TG183(B) 47
   TG184, TG185 48
   TG185, TG 186 50
tooling 25, 35
   carbon-based 27
   female 26, 47, 55, 60, 62, 66, 82,
      86, 87, 102, 108
   glass-fibre based 27, 32, 81

male 26, 72, 75
resins 27, 77
split 49
two-piece 25
torsion boxes 60, 62
turbo inlet duct 47
two-component adhesives 17
two-piece tooling 25
two-stage cure 34
TWR 61–65

U
UFO 2 59–60
underbody 54, 73
under-diffuser duct 86
undertrays 40, 47, 77, 90
underwings 46, 81, 87

V
vacuum-bag 25, 31, 34, 35, 62, 75
   disposable 31
   method 25
vacuum curing 25, 34
vacuum take-off points 32
venturi underbodies 66

W
Walkinshaw, Tom 61, 63
Warwick, Derek 63
weave types (fibre) 21
West Zakspeed 41
wet lay-up method 13, 27
Wheatley, Chris 117
Wheatley Lingham 500 117–118
wheel covers 62
Williams, Frank 94
Williams GP Engineering 87–94
   FW06, FW07B/C, FW08/C,
      FW09/B 87
   FW10/B 88
   FW11 92
wings 66, 80
   end plates 77, 86, 87
   front 47, 82, 86, 87
   front spar 48
   rear 49, 83, 86, 87
Wolf 39, 54
wooden chassis 16
world land-speed record 42, 44

Y
Yamaha 98, 100, 101